Communicate in Writing

A functional approach to writing through reading comprehension

Keith Johnson

Centre for Applied Language Studies
University of Reading

for Tanya

Longman

Contents

Part 1 Describing things and ideas

Part 2 Describing processes and events

Part 3 Developing an argument

Part 1

Describing things and ideas

Unit 1 (Introductory Unit)

Introduction to 'Communicate in Writing'

1. Note-taking

Read this passage about '*Communicate in Writing*'. Following it are some notes on Paragraphs 1 and 2. Copy and complete them. Write in your own books.

'*Communicate in Writing*' has been written for two types of student. One is the student who is learning English in order to study some other subject, in the arts or sciences, and who wants to learn how to write academic English. The other is the student whose main interest is English and who needs to learn how to write essays as part of his school or university course.

As its title suggests, the book's main aim is to teach writing. But each unit contains a passage of English, followed by exercises to make sure you have understood how that passage is organised. There is, in other words, quite a lot of reading practice. Why is so much reading practice given in a book on writing? Simply because if you wish to organise your own essays correctly, it is important to understand how other writers have organised their passages. Answering questions like 'How is this passage organised?' and 'In what other ways could the writer have organised it?' is a useful step towards improving your own writing.

Each unit of '*Communicate in Writing*' is about a different subject. Unit 2 for example is about stars and planets, and Unit 5 is about volcanoes. These subjects have been chosen because of their general interest, and you do not have to be an expert on each subject to follow the units. Even so, the student who is learning English in order to study some other subject may ask whether he would spend his time better reading and writing about his own subject. This is not necessarily true. Essays, reports and dissertations have a lot in common, whether they are about zoology, chemistry or sociology. So the zoologist, the chemist and the sociologist can learn a lot about writing good English by reading and writing passages on subjects of general interest. There is a glossary at the back of the book to help you with unfamiliar words. Words in the glossary are marked with an asterisk (*).

1. 2 types of student: (a) Student learning Eng. to study other subject. . . . .
   (b) . . . .
2. Book teaches . . . . . . But much . . . . . . practice in it.
   Reason: . . . . . .

2. Understanding the passage

Does the writer believe these things? Read Paragraph 3 and decide:

(a) The student can learn by reading and writing about subjects other than his own subject.

(b) The student would spend his time better reading and writing about his own subject.

(c) Essays on different subjects are very different from each other.

(d) You can use '*Communicate in Writing*' without knowing a lot about the subjects discussed in each unit.

3. 'Even so'

(i) The expression 'even so' means 'in spite of this'. Find the example of this expression in the passage. Write a sentence making the same point, but beginning 'in spite of the fact that . . .'

(ii) Use the information given in the passage to complete these sentences:

(a) As its title suggests, the book teaches writing. Even so, ...

(b) There are some differences between essays on different subjects. Even so, ...

(c) . . . . . . ; even so, the book's main aim is to teach writing.

(d) . . . . . . ; even so, you do not have to be an expert on each subject to follow the units.

4. Completing a passage

Originally the passage had a fourth paragraph describing how '*Communicate in Writing*' is organised. Use the information given on the contents page (page ii) to complete this part of the paragraph. (Sometimes a space needs more than one word.) Write in your own books.

'*Communicate in Writing*' is divided into . . . . . . parts. The first ten units are about . . . . . . ; Units 11–15 deal with . . . . . . , and Units . . . . . . with developing an argument. There are three different . . . . Unit 1 is an introductory unit, and . . . . . . to introduce the student to the book. Units 5, 10, 15, 20 are . . . . . . , and contain revision exercises. . . . . . . are main units.

5. The main units

The paragraph ends by describing how each main unit is organised. Here are some notes on what the writer says. Finish the paragraph:

Main Units

3 parts.
1. Passage + exercises associated with passage.
2. An important aspect of writing (e.g. Unit 3 'defining'; Unit 4 'classifying'.)
3. Additional exercises – to be done if there is time.

Unit 2

Dying stars ... and living planets

Part I

1. Read this passage about dying stars, and complete the table which follows it. Write in your own books.

The old belief that the universe never changes is quite wrong. Even before the invention of the telescope*, astronomers* noticed that bright stars suddenly appear in the sky, and then later disappear. These stars were called 'novae' because they were thought to be new. In fact we now know that they are really old stars which are slowly dying. A recent case of a nova occurred in 1918, and one of the few people who saw this was the American astronomer Edward Barnard. He was driving along in a car, occasionally looking up into the sky. Suddenly he noticed a star that he had never seen before, and exclaimed, 'That star should not be there!' He was in fact watching the explosion of a nova.

Novae are old stars which are slowly dying. As they do so, they let out* huge clouds of material, sometimes as large as the earth, and these explode into space at a speed of about 8,000,000 kilometres per hour. When this happens, the hotter parts of the star become visible, and this is why novae are so bright. Although the explosions are huge on a human scale, they only consume* a small part of the dying star's energy. The death is a slow one, and the star may continue to explode for thousands of years. Indeed, there are even some stars which explode once a fortnight.

There are other old stars which do not die slowly, but are completely destroyed by one great explosion. These are known as 'supernovae'. The explosion of a supernova is equivalent to about a million, million, million, million hydrogen bombs going off* at the same time. Just before the explosion the star's density* becomes very great and it spins at a very high speed. A matchbox of material taken from the star at that time would weigh about 1,000 tons, and the star would be turning at about 16,000,000 kilometres per hour. The explosion itself occurs suddenly, in the space of a minute, but the supernova continues to shine long after the event. One supernova which Chinese astronomers observed in 1054 can still be seen by us today. It has been shining for at least nine hundred years.

NOVAE	SUPERNOVAE
1. die slowly	1. die suddenly . . . .
2. many explosions	2. . . . .
3. each explosion destroys one small part only	3. . . . .
4.	4. shine continuously for long time

2. Note-taking

(i) Complete these notes on Paragraph 1. Write the missing words in your own books:

. . . . does change. Bright . . . . suddenly appear, then disappear. Called '. . . . . . .' because thought . . . . In fact, old stars slowly . . . . Recent case* occurred in . . . .

(ii) Notes should be short, so that you can read them quickly later. They need not be grammatical, and you can leave out articles ('the', 'a', 'some'), etc. But they must be complete enough for you to understand. Make these notes on Paragraph 2 shorter. Then show them to your partner. Can he understand them?

Novae = old stars which are slowly dying.
They are bright because the hotter parts of the star become visible as they explode and let out huge clouds of material. The death is slow, so the star may continue to explode for thousands of years.

3. Referring back

Words like 'this', 'these', 'it', 'so' usually *refer back* to something the writer has already mentioned. Decide what these words in the passage refer back to:

line 13 This = (a) the great speed (b) letting out clouds of material (c) the slow death of old stars
line 14 This = (a) letting out clouds of material (b) the hotter parts (c) the exposure* of the hotter parts
line 20 These = (a) the great explosions (b) the old stars destroyed by one explosion (c) old stars
line 23 It = (a) the star (b) the star's density (c) the explosion
line 11 So = (a) let out clouds of material (b) explode (c) slowly die

10►

Dying stars ... and living planets

4. Novae and supernovae

In Exercise 1 you completed a table showing the differences between 'novae' and 'supernovae'. Write a short paragraph describing these differences.

Part II Referring back, and giving new information

Except when they are introducing a completely new subject, most sentences *refer back* to something already mentioned. At the same time, they usually say something new. They *give new information*.

Very often it is the *first part* of the sentence which refers back, and the *last part* which gives new information. For example:

> . . . which do not die slowly, but are completely destroyed by one great explosion. These are known as 'supernovae'.

The first word ('these') in the underlined sentence refers back to something already mentioned – the old stars destroyed by one great explosion. The rest of the sentence ('are known as "supernovae"') gives the reader new information.

5. In each of these examples from the passage, the first few (underlined) words refer back to something already mentioned. Decide what.

line 11 (a) As they do so, they let out huge clouds of material . . .
line 16 (b) The death is a slow one, . . .
line 26 (c) The explosion itself occurs suddenly . . .
line 28 (d) It has been shining . . .

6. The moon

Look at these sentences:

The time it takes the moon to orbit* is called the lunar month.

Twenty seven days	is	one lunar month.
NEW INFORMATION		REFERRING BACK

We can rewrite the second sentence so that the *first part* refers back and the *last part* gives new information:

The time it takes the moon to orbit is called the lunar month.

One lunar month	is	twenty seven days.
REFERRING BACK		NEW INFORMATION

Unit 2

Here are some more sentences about the moon, Earth's nearest neighbour. Rewrite them in the same way.

(a) At the equator* the moon's temperature reaches 28°C. The hottest part of the moon is of course the equator.

(b) Some of the craters* of the moon are very large. The same structure is seen in the large and small craters.

(c) The lunar month is getting longer. The moon is moving farther away, so the lunar month is getting longer.

(d) The moon does not have any light of its own. The sun shines its light onto the moon.

(e) The moon is a great ball of rock. The earth is eighty times the size of the moon.

11 ▶

7. The death of our sun

Novae and supernovae are millions of miles away. Much more important to us (in about 10,000,000,000 years' time!) is the death of our own sun. Here is what will happen:

Sun gets much hotter. The oceans of the earth are boiled by the sun.

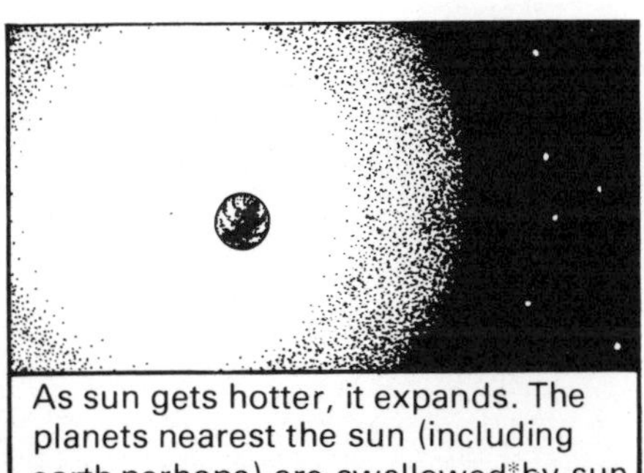

As sun gets hotter, it expands. The planets nearest the sun (including earth perhaps) are swallowed* by sun.

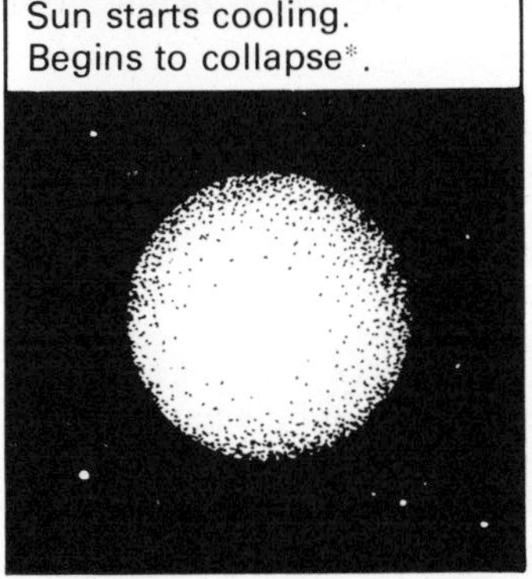

Sun starts cooling. Begins to collapse*.

Sun changes colour, from red to blue to white. Sun's light goes out completely.

The sun and planets are dead.

Write a paragraph about the death of the sun and the planets. Remember what you have studied about referring back and giving new information. Use words like 'this', 'it' and 'so' to refer back.

8. Parallel writing

(i) The largest planet of our sun is Jupiter. Here is a short passage describing Jupiter:

The planet Jupiter is fifth nearest to the sun, the distance between the two being 483 million miles. It spins very rapidly, taking only 9 hours 50 minutes to complete one rotation*. With a diameter* of 89,000 miles, Jupiter is the largest of the planets; it is also very heavy – much heavier than the earth. Because it is so far from the sun, Jupiter's surface is very cold and can reach temperatures as low as −138°C. Its 'atmosphere' is mostly hydrogen and helium*.

In what order does the writer describe these things?
diameter; 'atmosphere'; weight; distance from sun; temperature; speed of rotation.

(ii) Now here is some information about another planet, Venus. It is sometimes called the 'mysterious planet', because we know so little about it.

VENUS: the 'mysterious planet'

'Atmosphere': 95% carbon dioxide
Diameter: 7,700 miles (one of the smallest planets)
Weight: not great; about same as earth
Distance from sun: 67 million miles (second nearest planet to sun)
Temperature: very hot; as high as 477°C
Speed of rotation: we don't know, but probably very slow – between 68 hours and 250 days for one rotation!

Write a passage about Venus. Make it look as much like the Jupiter description as possible. Describe the same things, in the same order. Begin: 'The planet Venus is second nearest to the sun . . .'

12▶

9. Writing about your subject

Write a paragraph describing your subject for someone who knows nothing about it. Show the description to someone in the class (if possible someone who is studying another subject). Can the person understand what you have written? If not, make your description clearer.

Part III Additional exercises

10. Adding information

You want to add this information to Paragraph 3 of the passage. Decide *where* you would put it, and *what words* you would use.

(a) The explosion of a supernova is like a cosmic bomb.

(b) The supernova which the Chinese saw is known today as the Crab Nebula.

(c) The records of the Royal Observatory in Peking mention the Crab Nebula supernova.

(d) Supernovae can shine for well over a thousand years.

11. Describing the moon

Use the information given in Exercise 6 to write a short description of the moon.

12. Comparing Jupiter and Venus

Use the information in Exercise 8 to write a passage *comparing* Jupiter and Venus.

Further reading

Moore P. *The New Look of the Universe*, Zenith Books, 1966.
Hoyle F. *The Nature of the Universe*, Penguin Books, 1963.
Gamow G. *A Star Called the Sun*, Penguin Books, 1967.

Unit 3

Skid row

Part I

1. Read this passage about skid row, and complete the table which follows it. Write in your own books.

Vagrancy has long been a problem in both Europe and America. Indeed, the first mention of the problem in Britain was made in A.D. 368. Vagrants – people, that is, not living in one fixed place but moving from town to town – have always been severely punished by the law; more severely in many countries than drunks or beggars. 'Everyone', the law says, 'must have a bedroom.'

In Europe there have never been places where vagrants can collect together in a community. In fact governments have often tried to solve the problem by returning vagrants to the place where they were born. In this way they have prevented large communities of vagrants from forming. But in America, such communities have been allowed to collect in almost every city. These communities are known as 'skid row'. Skid row is something found only in the United States. It is the area of an American city in which the homeless live. The expression was originally 'skid road'. It was the name given to the road in Seattle down which trees were pushed (or 'skidded'*) after they had been cut down. The lumberjacks who had cut the trees down lived along this road. The word 'road' changed to 'row', and now the expression 'skid row' is used for any vagrant community in America.

The vagrant's main problem is to find a place to sleep. There are different types of accommodation on skid row. The best is in 'tourist hotels'. These are quite clean and try to give some protection against fire and theft. Much worse are the 'flophouses', public or private houses which give the vagrant a floor to sleep on. But the worst accommodation of all is found in the 'hobo jungle'. This is an area of skid row consisting of a few shacks – small houses made of pieces of metal, wood and even cardboard*.

WORD	DEFINITION
1. vagrant	1. person moving from town to town
2.	2. men who cut down trees
3. flophouse	3. . . . .
4. hobo jungle	4. . . . .
5.	5. house made of metal, wood, cardboard

2. Understanding the passage

Which of these sentences best describes the writer's *main point*:

In Paragraph 1 the writer:

(a) compares punishments for vagrancy, drunkenness and begging.
(b) says that vagrancy has long been a problem.
(c) gives a short history of vagrancy.

In Paragraph 2 the writer:

(a) introduces and talks about the idea of skid row.
(b) gives the origins of the expression 'skid row'.
(c) describes different solutions to the problem of vagrancy.

How would you describe the *main point* the writer makes in Paragraph 3?

3. Note-taking and summarising

(i) Complete these notes on Paragraph 3. Write in your own books:

Skid row accommodation

(a) . . . tourist hotels . . . . : quite clean + give some protection — Best
(b) . . . . : . . . . ↓
(c) . . . . : . . . . Worst

(ii) Here is a summary of the passage with some words missing. What do you think the missing words might be? (One word per space.) Write in your own books.

Vagrancy, ... a problem in many countries, has always been . . . . . . punished by the law. European . . . . . . have often tried to solve the problem . . . . . . returning vagrants to . . . . . . birthplace, ... in America vagrant communities called skid rows have grown up in . . . . . . every city. The vagrants on skid row . . . . . . in different types of accommodation, from the fairly clean and . . . . . . 'tourist hotels' down to the 'hobo jungle', ... of a few shacks.

4. Adding information

You want to add these sentences to the passage, one to each paragraph. What do the words 'this' and 'these' refer to? Decide *where* you would put them.

(a) Some of these are tolerable, while others are extremely bad.
(b) But in spite of this, vagrancy is still a problem.
(c) This was, for example, the solution tried in 17th century England.

5. More practice in referring back

In Unit 2 you saw how the *first part* of a sentence often refers back, and the *second part* gives new information. Some of the sentences below do not begin by referring back. Which? How would you rewrite them?

(a) These communities are known as 'skid row'. America has communities known as 'skid row'.

(b) It was the road in Seattle down which trees were pushed. Along this road lived the lumberjacks.

(c) The best accommodation is in 'tourist hotels'. Protection against fire and theft is given in tourist hotels.

(d) Much worse are the 'flophouses'. Flophouses give no more than a floor to sleep on.

Part II Defining

6.

(i) Here is how the writer defines skid row:

> Skid row is the area of an American city in which the homeless live.

Use the table you completed in Exercise 1 to make more definitions like this.

(ii) Notice the structures the writer of the passage uses to define the words in the table.

7. Here is another way of defining skid row:

> The area of an American city in which the homeless live is known as skid row.

Use the table to make five more definitions like this.

8. When can you use these two types of definition? Decide whether (a) or (b) would follow each underlined sentence. Remember what you have learned about *referring back* and *giving new information*.

<u>Some people in America do not live in one fixed place</u>.

(a) Vagrants are people who do not live in one fixed place.
(b) People who do not live in one fixed place are known as vagrants.

There are many vagrants in America.

(a) Vagrants are people who do not live in one fixed place.
(b) People who do not live in one fixed place are known as vagrants.

Some people in skid row live in shacks.

(a) The area of skid row which consists of shacks is known as the 'hobo jungle'.
(b) The 'hobo jungle' is an area of skid row which consists of shacks.

Every skid row has a hobo jungle.

(a) The area of skid row which consists of shacks is known as the 'hobo jungle'.
(b) 'Hobo jungle' is an area of skid row which consists of shacks.

9. Adding information

The people who live on skid row have their own way of talking, their own slang*. Here is a passage which uses some of their slang expressions. Guess what these expressions might mean:

Some vagrants are bundle stiffs who travel from one skid row to another by rattler. But most (about 80%) are homeguards. Once the homeguard has somewhere to sleep, his next problem is to find food. He can take food from the missionaries*, but if he can afford it he will always prefer to eat in a beanery. Sometimes he will work as a beanery pearl diver, receiving food rather than money for his work.

The meaning of the slang expressions is given at the bottom of the page. Rewrite the passage making their meaning clear. Use some of the structures you noticed in Exercise 6 (ii).

13▶

10. Parallel writing

Many different sorts of people live on skid row. Here are descriptions of two of them:

The 'Wino'

The skid row wino is a type of drunk. But he differs from the 'normal' drunk in one important way. He does not drink because he is addicted*, but because drinking a lot is the habit on skid row. Nor is the wino an alcoholic, and he behaves quite differently. The alcoholic often drinks alone, and the

---

Beanery – a restaurant on skid row which sells very cheap food
Bundle stiff – vagrant who carries his own bed (usually a blanket) with him
Homeguard – vagrant who stays on same skid row all year
Pearl diver – one who washes dishes in a restaurant
Rattler – a train carrying freight*

wino always drinks with groups of friends. Also, the wino likes to be drunk for as long as possible. The alcoholic on the other hand gets drunk as quickly as possible, and then stops drinking for a time. The wino is, then, a drunk without an addiction to alcohol; he drinks with groups of friends, and likes to be drunk for as long as possible.

The 'Panhandler'

The panhandler begs in order to buy alcohol; he asks for money, and will ask anyone, even another person on skid row. He is a type of beggar, but he only asks for money – unlike the 'scavenger'* who collects objects which he then sells. Another difference between the scavenger and the panhandler is that other people on skid row do not like the scavenger. But they help the panhandler because they understand his need. The panhandler is also different from most 'normal' beggars. They beg to earn money; he begs so that he can afford to drink.

(i) In the first passage the writer:

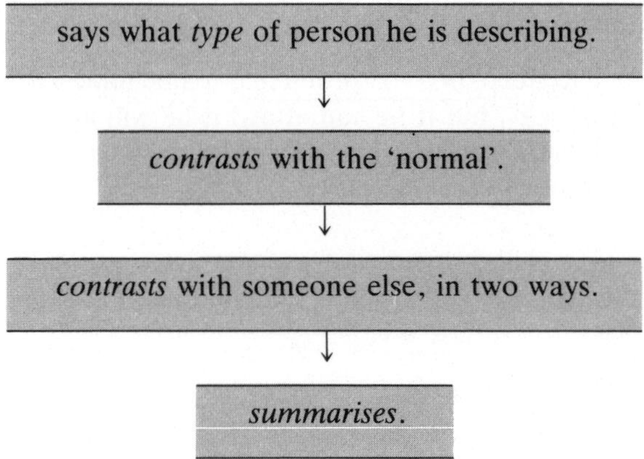

In what order does the writer of the second passage do these things?

(ii) Rewrite the 'panhandler' description to look as much like the 'wino' description as possible. Begin: 'The skid row panhandler is a type of . . .'

14▶

11. Writing about your subject

Write a paragraph defining an important idea (or thing) associated with your subject. Write so that someone who knows nothing about your subject will understand. Show the paragraph to someone in the class. Does the person understand your definition? If not, make it clearer.

Part III Additional exercises

12. Reorganising a paragraph

In the passage the writer describes the origin of the expression 'skid row'. Rewrite his description beginning like this:

The expression was originally 'skid road'. It was the name given to a road along which lumberjacks . . .

13. Rewrite the passage in Exercise 9 so that it contains no slang expressions at all.

14. Skid row types

Here are some notes on the paragraph which follows the passage on page 10. Write the paragraph yourself.

Types of people on skid row

(a) Wino. Much drinking in groups. Drunkenness normal.
(b) Tramps*. Wander from place to place. Rare today. Most skid rowers are homeguards.
(c) Beggars, e.g. panhandlers and scavengers.
(d) 'Mission stiffs'. Persons living on charity* from missionaries. Hated by other skid rowers (because they take charity).

Further reading

Wallace S. E. *Skid Row as a Way of Life*, The Bedminister Press, 1965.
Rowland J. *Community Decay*, Penguin Books, 1973. (For those interested in urban problems in Britain)
Murphy R. E. *The American City*, McGraw-Hill, 1966.
Cook T. *Vagrant Alcoholics*, Routledge and Kegan Paul, 1975.

Unit 4

Bees ... and things that crawl*

Part I

1. Read this passage about bees, and complete the diagram which follows it. Write in your own books.

It is a common theme in many science fiction stories that the world may one day be taken over* by insects. There are certainly a very large number of insect species* on earth. Indeed, about 700,000 species have so far been described, and about 70% of all the animal species we know of are insects.

The most intelligent family of insects are the Hymenoptera. These are insects which, at some time in their life, have two pairs of transparent* wings. Hymenoptera may be classified according to whether or not they have a 'waist'*. Those which have a waist are known as petiolate, and those which do not are called sessileventres. There are two types of petiolata: the parasites* (parasitica) and the stinging* insects (aculeata). Bees belong to the second category.

We usually think of bees as being sociable insects which live in large communities, but this is not always true. One way of classifying bees is into 'social' and 'solitary' species, and there are many of the latter. Bumble bees and honey bees are social species. One important difference between these two is that the bumble bee has a much longer tongue. It can fertilise* plants which the honey bee's tongue cannot even reach. It has been said that the bumble bee won the Boer War! The horses that helped to win that war fed on clover*, a plant which only the bumble bee can fertilise. Without the bumble bee there would be no clover.

There are three types of individual in the bumble bee community – the large female who is fertile* (the Queen); the many infertile* females (the workers) and the few males, or 'drones'. Unlike nearly all other insects, the Queen actually sits on her eggs like a chicken. As soon as they are born, the workers begin collecting food. They continue to work throughout their short life. It is overwork which eventually kills them.

Unit 4

Classification of Hymenoptera

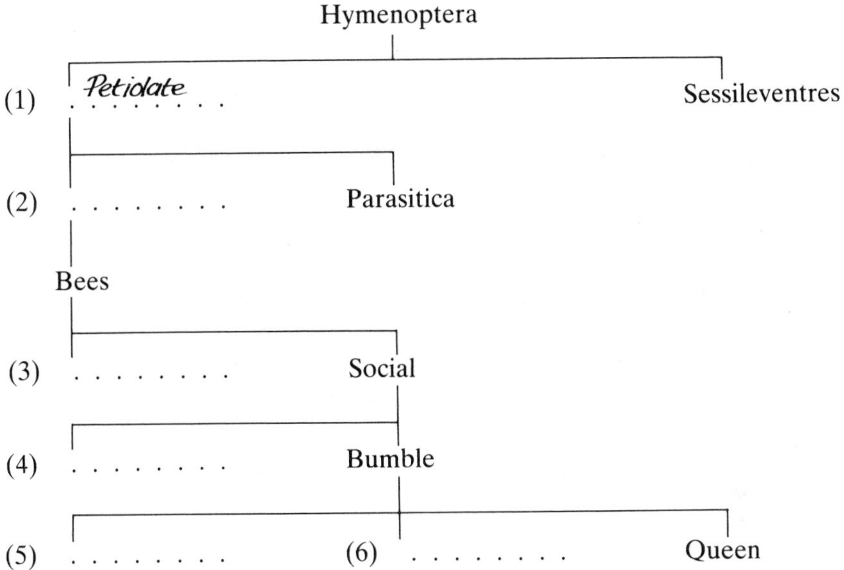

2. Note-taking

Here are some notes a student has taken on Paragraphs 1 and 2 of the passage. He has made four mistakes. Decide what they are, then rewrite the notes in a correct and shorter form.

Paragraph 1 Very large number of insect species –

80% of all animal species we know of are insects.
700,000 species of insect have so far been described.

Paragraph 2 Hymenoptera – all at some time in their life have a pair of transparent wings

(a) Sessileventres – these have a waist.
(b) Petiolata – these do not have a waist:
 (i) Parasites. For example, bees.
 (ii) Stinging insects.

3. Vocabulary extension

Here are some expressions that could have been used in Paragraph 3, to make it a little more formal and academic. Decide where each expression could be used. Use a dictionary if necessary.

(i) accustomed to thinking
(ii) the case
(iii) these distinguished themselves in that
(iv) this enables it to
(v) claimed
(vi) if it were not for

4. Sentence combining

Here are some of the main points the writer makes in the passage. Join the sentences together to make a summary of the passage:

(1) There are a very large number of insect species on earth.
(2) The most intelligent species are the Hymenoptera.
(3) Hymenoptera have two pairs of transparent wings at some time in their life.
(4) Bees are members of the Hymenoptera family.
(5) Bees are stinging insects.
(6) Some bees are solitary.
(7) Bumble and honey bees are social species.
(8) Every bumble bee community has a Queen.
(9) The Queen is fertile.
(10) Every bumble bee community has workers and drones.

5. Supporting a statement

One use of the word 'indeed' is to introduce a sentence which *supports* a statement that has just been made. Find an example of this use of 'indeed' in the passage. What is the statement being supported?

Here are some sentences from the passage. Is the word 'indeed' being used correctly? If so, what is the statement being supported?

line 25 (a) They continue to work through their short life. Indeed, it is overwork which eventually kills them.

line 5 (b) The most intelligent family of insects are the Hymenoptera. Indeed, they are all insects which, at some time in their life, have two pairs of transparent wings.

line 15 (c) One important difference between these two is that the bumble bee has a much longer tongue. Indeed, it can fertilise plants which the honey bee's tongue cannot reach.

line 23 (d) Unlike nearly all other insects, the Queen actually sits on her eggs like a chicken. Indeed, as soon as they are born, the workers begin collecting food.

line 18 (e) The horses that helped to win that war fed on clover, a plant which only the bumble bee can fertilise. Indeed, without bumble bees there would be no clover.

Part II Classifying

6. Here is the sentence from the passage which classifies petiolata:

> There are two types of petiolata: the parasites (parasitica) and the stinging insects (aculeata).

Use the table you completed in Exercise 1 to classify Hymenoptera, bees, social bees and bumble bees in the same way.

7. Now look at how the writer classifies Hymenoptera:

> Hymenoptera may be classified according to whether or not they have a 'waist'. Those which have a waist are known as petiolata, and those which do not are called sessileventres.

In the first sentence the writer tells us his *criterion* for classifying.
In the second he *names* the classes, and gives a *short description* of each.

(i) Write a classification of *female bumble bees* which has the same structure.

(ii) To most people insects are very much alike. Do you know what the difference between these insects is? The answers are given at the bottom of the page.

(a) Butterflies and moths. (b) Locusts* and grasshoppers*.
(c) Wasps* and bees.

Now classify Lepidoptera, Orthoptera saltatoria and aculeata. Give your criterion for classifying. Name and describe the classes.

8. Bee dances

A famous German scientist, Karl von Frisch, has studied the way bees communicate with each other. He discovered that they have a complicated system of communication using dances. Here are some of the bee dances we know about:

(a) Butterflies fly by day and moths fly at night. They are both members of the Lepidoptera order.
(b) Locusts migrate* while grasshoppers do not. They are both Orthoptera saltatoria.
(c) Wasps are carnivorous (eating other insects). Bees are not. They are both aculeata.

'Jostling* Dance'
Tells the bees food has been found. The food is good.

'Tail Wagging* Dance'
Tells the bees where the food is. It is a long way away.

'Round Dance'
Tells the bees where the food is. It is nearby.

'Trembling* Dance'
Tells the bees food has been found. But the food is poisonous.

How can these dances be classified? Use the information to write a classification, like this:

There are two sorts of bee dance associated with food: those that tell the bees . . . . . . , and those that tell the bees . . . . In this first category are the '. . . . . . Dance' and the '. . . . . . Dance'. The first of these informs the bees . . . . . . , while the second . . . . The second category of dance indicates . . . . Of this type the '. . . . . .' tells the bees . . . . The '. . . . . . Dance' on the other hand . . . .

12 ▶

9. Spiders

(i) Here is part of an informal talk given to a small group of students. It is about spiders. Read the talk and write a table like the one you completed in Exercise 1.

Well today I'm going to talk to you about spiders. Now spiders aren't insects at all. That's because they have eight legs, and proper insects have only six. So what are spiders? Well, there's a very large group of animals called arthropodae. All these arthropodae have one thing in common – thick skins like shells*. You can see this most clearly in the beetles*. Anyway, some of this big group live in water, and we call them crustacea. Crabs*, lobsters* and shrimps* are crustacea. Other arthropodae live in air, and these are called tracheata. There are three sorts of these. One group has many legs – the myriopods, like centipedes* and millipedes*. Then there are the insects, which have six legs as I've said. The third group are spiders, or arachnidae to give them their scientific name. Now, we always think of spiders as spinning* webs*, and in fact all spiders can spin. But they don't all catch their food in their webs. Those who do are called 'trappers'* – they just spin a web and wait for their food to come to them, like a fisherman. But there is another big group of spiders called 'hunters'*. They go out and find their food. There are three sorts of these. The crab spiders are the cleverest. They hide and wait for the food to come close. Then they attack. Then there are the wolf spiders, and the most famous of these is the tarantula*. Wolf spiders move very quickly, and that's how they catch their food. Then there's another interesting collection of spiders called jumping spiders. They jump on their food. Sometimes they jump from a wall into the air to catch a flying insect. They don't fall because they are attached to a thread*, like someone climbing a mountain . . .

(ii) The editor of a nature journal asks the speaker to write up his talk as an article. The style must be quite formal and scientific. How do you think he writes up the part about spiders (line 10 onwards)?

13▶

10. Writing about your subject

Write a paragraph classifying something associated with your subject. Write so that someone who knows nothing about your subject will understand the paragraph. Show it to someone in the class. If they don't understand what you've written, make it clearer.

Part III Additional exercises

11. Reorganising a paragraph

Paragraph 2 of the passage on page 16 begins by talking about Hymenoptera, and finishes by talking about bees. Rewrite the paragraph so that it begins by talking about bees, and finishes by talking about Hymenoptera. Make this your opening sentence:
'Bees are stinging insects, or aculeata.'

12. More bee dances

Not all bee dances are associated with food. Here are two more dances von Frisch describes:

'Buzzing Dance' – tells the bees to collect together
'Shaking Dance' – the dancer is asking to be washed by the other bees

Add sentences to the paragraph you wrote in Exercise 8 so that it classifies all the bee dances – associated with food and not associated with food.

13. Jumping spiders

Imagine you want to write a passage about jumping spiders. In order to introduce your subject you decide to write a *short* introductory paragraph about arthropodae in general, and mentioning other sorts of spiders. Write this introductory paragraph.

Bees ... and things that crawl

Further reading

von Frisch K. *The Dancing Bees*, Methuen, 1954.
Wilson E. O. *The Insect Societies*, The Belknap Press of Harvard, 1971.
Step E. *British Insect Life*, T. Werner Laurie, 1935.
Bristowe W. S. *The World of Spiders*, Collins, 1958.

Unit 5 (Consolidation Unit)

Volcanoes

Part I

1. Completing a passage

Read this passage about volcanoes. Some words (and sometimes whole sentences) are missing from it. Write down in your own books what you think the missing words might be.

Together with earthquakes, volcanoes are phenomena which both delight and terrify the human mind at the same time. Some of the most beautiful mountains in the world, admired by all who see them, (1) . . . . On the other hand, volcanoes have throughout history (2) . . . . The term volcano is associated with the island of Vulcano, just north of Sicily. (3) . . . . , this was thought to be the home of the god Vulcan – the god of destruction. Volcanoes have always been objects of mystery, and (4) . . . . . . even despite the advances of science.

A volcano is a kind of chimney, or 'vent' which goes down to a liquid deep inside the earth, called 'magma'. (5) . . . . . . of material come out of this vent: a hot liquid called lava, pieces of rock, and great quantities of gas. The lava and rock often collect round the vent and form what is known as the volcano's 'cone'. Volcanic eruptions (6) . . . . In one, the lava comes quietly to the surface and flows away as a river, causing little damage except to objects directly in its path. On the other extreme great explosions occur, frequently blowing away the cone and causing great damage. (7) . . . . . . are intermediate between these two extremes.

(8) . . . . . . This is usually done according to the type of vent or the nature of the explosion. According to this latter classification, the most explosive type of volcano is the Peléan type, (9) . . . . . . the eruption of Mount Pelée in the Lesser Antibes in 1902. (10) . . . . . . is the so-called 'nuée ardente' or 'glowing cloud'. This is a great cloud of red lava thrown from the volcano at high speed.

2. Here is the completed passage. Compare your words with the original ones, and discuss any differences. Then complete the diagram which follows. Write in your own books.

Together with earthquakes*, volcanoes* are phenomena which both delight and terrify the human mind at the same time. Some of the most beautiful mountains in the world, admired* by all who see them, are volcanoes. On the other hand, volcanoes have throughout history caused great destruction. The term volcano is associated with the island of Vulcano, just north of Sicily. In classical times, this was thought to be the home of the god Vulcan – the god of destruction. Volcanoes have always been objects of mystery, and this is true today even despite the advances of science.

A volcano is a kind of chimney, or 'vent' which goes down to a liquid deep inside the earth, called 'magma'. Three types of material come out of this vent: a hot liquid called lava, pieces of rock, and great quantities of gas. The lava and rock often collect round the vent and form what is known as the volcano's 'cone'*. Volcanic eruptions* vary between two extremes. In one, the lava comes quietly to the surface and flows* away as a river, causing little damage except to objects directly in its path. On the other extreme great explosions occur, frequently blowing away* the cone and causing great damage. The great majority of the world's volcanoes are intermediate between these two extremes.

There are several ways of classifying volcanoes. This is usually done according to the type of vent or the nature of the explosion. According to this latter classification, the most explosive type of volcano is the Peléan type, named after the eruption of Mount Pelée in the Lesser Antibes in 1902. The characteristic feature of this type is the so-called 'nuée ardente' or 'glowing* cloud'. This is a great cloud of red lava thrown from the volcano at high speed.

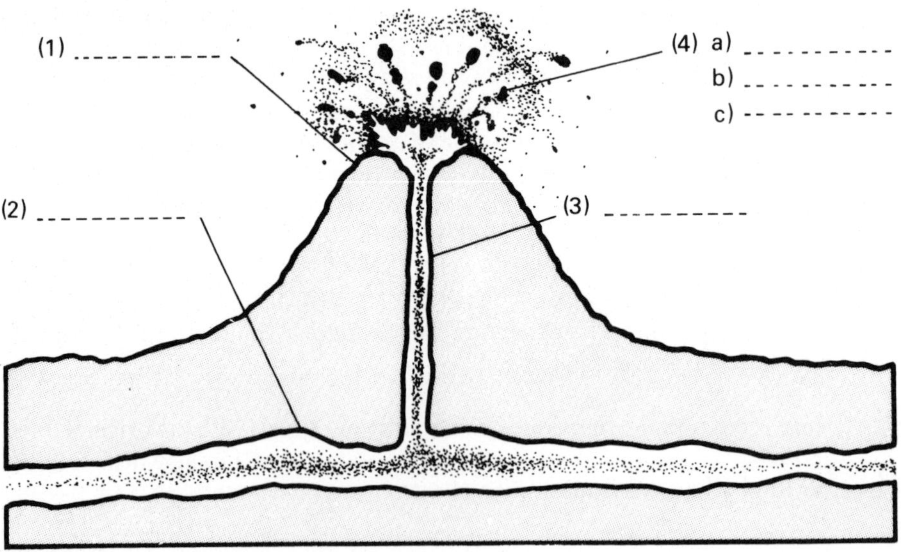

3. Revision

In Unit 3 you practised defining difficult words. Choose five difficult words from the passage, and add phrases to the sentences in which they appear to make their meanings clear.

4. Understanding the passage

In which order does the writer of the passage make these points? Organise this plan so that the order is correct.

Paragraph 1

(a) derivation* of the word volcano.
(b) why volcanoes terrify us.
(c) the mystery of volcanoes.
(d) why volcanoes delight us.

Paragraph 2

(a) general types of volcanic eruption.
(b) definition of a volcano.
(c) materials coming out of a volcano.
(d) definition of a cone.

Paragraph 3

(a) name of the most explosive type of volcano.
(b) ways of classifying volcanoes.
(c) characteristics of the Peléan volcano.

5. Other volcano types

Paragraph 3 continues with descriptions of other volcano types. Use these notes to complete the paragraph. First decide in which order you will describe the different types.

Strombolean type:

e.g. Stromboli volcano, to north of Sicily. Characteristic is frequent regular explosions. Not very explosive.

Vulcanian type:

Almost as explosive as Peléan, but no 'nuée ardente'. Characteristic is dark cloud shaped like cabbage*, e.g. Vesuvius in Italy.

Icelandic type:

Lava comes out quietly. Least explosive type, e.g. Mount Hekla in Iceland.

Part II Beginning a description

The volcano passage is the *beginning* of a long essay about volcanoes. It contains:

- something about the history of the subject*, including a derivation (of the word 'volcano')
- a definition
- classifications

Many *opening paragraphs of descriptions* contain these things.

6. The destruction of volcanoes

Imagine you want to write an opening paragraph for an essay on volcanoes. In it, you wish to *emphasise the idea that volcanoes are destructive*, at the same time including something about history, a definition and a classification. Plan the paragraph, then write it.

7. Volcanoes and human life

Another way of *beginning a description* is to:

- state what your topic is
- tell the reader what points are going to be made, in which order

You want to write an essay about 'the effects volcanoes can have on human life'. Here are some things you could discuss:

- how we can predict volcanic eruptions
- the rich earth volcanic lava gives
- the destruction volcanoes can do
- how people can be protected against volcanic eruptions

Decide in which order you will do these things. Then write a short *opening paragraph*, stating your topic and telling the reader what points you are going to make, in which order.

Compare your paragraph with your partner's. Is he going to make the points in a different order? Discuss any differences.

8. Writing about your subject

Plan an essay describing an idea or thing associated with your own subject. Then write an *opening paragraph*. State your topic and tell the reader how you have organised your essay. If possible say something about history, and include a definition and a classification.

Give your paragraph to someone in the class. Do they understand what your essay is to be about, and how you have organised it? If not, make the paragraph clearer.

Further reading

Volcano: ordeal by fire in Iceland's Westmann Islands, Iceland Review, 1973. (For the story of one particular volcano)

Tazieff H. *Craters of Fire*, Hamilton, 1952.

Bullard F. M. *Volcanoes*, University of Texas Press and Nelson, 1962.

Oakeshott G. B. *Volcanoes and Earthquakes*, McGraw-Hill, 1976.

Unit 6

The polar regions

Part I

1. Read this passage about the polar regions*, then copy and complete the table which follows it.

The northern and southern polar regions are different in many ways. The most important difference concerns the distribution* of land and water. The northern Arctic regions are ice-covered sea, almost completely surrounded by land. The pole itself is in deep water. In the south, Antarctica is a huge continent* which is surrounded by a great ocean. Because of this basic difference other differences occur. The Arctic has a varied climate*, while the Antarctic climate varies little; the Arctic has much plant life but the Antarctic is an empty desert. And whereas the Arctic has been exploited* economically for centuries, trade* has never really touched Antarctica.

Interest in the Arctic began when America was discovered, and explorers* tried to find a western sea route to India and China. In their search to find the 'North-West Passage' the main problem facing the explorers was how to avoid the ice. One explorer, Nansen, found a unique answer to this problem. He deliberately became stuck in* the ice, and travelled with it across the Arctic Ocean! But although many explorers tried, it was not until 1903 that the Arctic polar region was crossed by sea. Antarctic exploration begins with Ptolemy. He believed that all the oceans were surrounded by land, and that therefore there was a huge continent somewhere in the south. His idea led to centuries of search, and again trade played its part. The real discoverers of Antarctica were the hunters who travelled far south to catch seals*.

One reason for the present interest in both polar regions is that the world may soon be short of fresh water. The world's population is doubling every 35 years, and in the United States alone an average person uses – taking everything into account – 1,500 gallons* of fresh water a day. The ice in the northern and southern polar regions is actually frozen fresh water. In fact over 85% of the earth's entire fresh water is found in the polar ice. If we could find a way of carrying this ice to other parts of the world, this would solve all our fresh water problems.

Arctic	Antarctic
1. ice-covered sea	1. huge continent
2. surrounded by land	2. . . . .
3.	3. pole lies on land
4. varied climate	4. . . . .
5. much plant life	5. . . . .
6.	6. no economic exploitation
7.	7. exploration begins with Ptolemy

2. Understanding the passage

Which of these sentences best describes the writer's *main point*?

In Paragraph 1 the writer:

(a) talks about differences in Arctic and Antarctic climate.
(b) says why the Arctic is more interesting than the Antarctic.
(c) contrasts the Arctic and Antarctic.

In Paragraph 2 the writer:

(a) describes the exploration of the polar regions.
(b) describes how the Arctic was first crossed.
(c) describes the importance of trade to exploration.

How would you describe the *main point* the writer makes in Paragraph 3?

3. Adding information

The passage was written by a student, and his tutor made these comments on Paragraph 3. How would you rewrite the paragraph to include these points?

(a) By the year 2000 the population of the world will be 6.3 billion*. At present it is 4 billion.

(b) You say the average American uses 1,500 gallons a day. Make it clear that this includes water used in making all the products* he uses. Also, you should say that in other countries the average person uses less fresh water than this.

(c) Say *why* the polar ice is fresh water. It's because these regions were once glaciers*. All glaciers are fresh water.

(d) Mention that many countries in the world (east and west) have recently been trying to carry ice.

The polar regions

4. 'Although'

(a) Although many explorers tried, the Arctic was not crossed by sea until 1903.

(b) Although the Arctic was not crossed by sea until 1903, many explorers tried.

(i) In one of these sentences, the writer's *main point* is that many explorers tried to cross the Arctic. In which sentence?
In the other, the *main point* is that the Arctic was not crossed by sea until 1903. In which sentence?
In these sentences, the *main points* are made in the *main clauses.**

(ii)

(a)	Although many explorers tried, the Arctic was not crossed by sea until 1903.	(b)	Although the Arctic was not crossed by sea until 1903, many explorers tried.

Nansen was one of them.

Which sentence, (a) or (b), comes before the underlined sentence? Why? The answer is given at the bottom of the page.

(iii) Now decide whether (a) or (b) comes before each underlined sentence.

(a) Although the Arctic is surrounded by land, the pole itself is in water.
(b) Although the pole itself is in water, the Arctic is surrounded by land.

The Antarctic is, on the other hand, surrounded by sea.

(a) Although the Arctic has been exploited, trade has never touched the Antarctic.
(b) Although trade has never touched the Antarctic, the Arctic has been exploited.

Indeed, it was discovered while trying to find a trade route to India and China.

(a) Although the Arctic has plant life, the Antarctic is an empty desert.
(b) Although the Antarctic is an empty desert, the Arctic has plant life.

Nor do many animals live there.

The answer is (b). The writer's *main points* are: Many explorers tried to cross the Arctic. Nansen was one of them.

(iv) Write sentences with 'although' to come before the underlined ones.

(a) [The Arctic has a varied climate.]
[The Antarctic climate varies little.]
In fact, there is little difference between summer and winter.

(b) [In some ways the polar regions are similar.]
[The polar regions are different in many ways.]
They are both, for example, extremely cold.

(c) [85% of the earth's fresh water is at the poles.]
[A way of carrying the water has not been found.]
In fact, according to some scientists, it is over 85%.

10▶

Part II Comparing and contrasting

In a *comparison* the writer emphasises similarities. In a *contrast* he emphasises differences.

5. Whereas the Arctic has been exploited economically for centuries, trade has never really touched Antarctica.

Use the table you completed in Exercise 1 to make more contrasts like this.

6. Completing a passage

Here are some expressions often used in comparisons. Use them to complete the passage:

as well as . . .
both . . .
like . . .
similar in . . .
both of . . .

Though there are differences between Arctic and Antarctic regions, they are . . . . . . one important respect*. . . . . . . them are old glaciers. This means that the ice in the Arctic . . . . . . Antarctica is in fact frozen fresh water. . . . . . . western countries, eastern countries are short of fresh water, and for this reason many countries of the world, ... east and west, have been trying to find ways of carrying the fresh water.

11▶

7. Polar climates

(a) Whereas the winter in Antarctica is longer and colder, both polar regions have long cold winters.

(b) Whereas both polar regions have long cold winters, the winter in Antarctica is longer and colder.

In (a) the writer mentions a difference between the polar regions, but in the main clause he is expressing a similarity. The sentence is a *comparison*. In (b) the writer mentions a similarity between the polar regions, but in the main clause he is emphasising a difference. The sentence is a *contrast*.

Here is some information about the climates of the polar regions. Make sentences like (a) and (b) above, comparing and contrasting.

Similarities and differences between polar climates

(Arc. = Arctic; Ant. = Antarctic)

SIMILARITIES	DIFFERENCES	OTHER DETAILS
Winter Both have long cold winters	Longer and colder in Ant.	Ant. temperature never higher than freezing*, can reach −70°F. Ant. colder because land.
Rain Little in either	More in Arc.	Arc. has rain in summer. Arc. 12 inches per year. 8″ in Ant.
Wind Both have strong winds	Stronger in Ant.	Ant. winds up to 190 m.p.h.* Average Ant. winds 5 times stronger than in Europe.
Fog* Both have much fog	More in Arc.	Arc. fog comes from surrounding sea. Very low fog.

Snow	
Both have much snow	In Ant. it does not often melt*. In Arc. melts in warm summer.

8. Comparing and contrasting climates

Work in pairs.
You write a paragraph mentioning similarities between polar climates, but emphasising their differences: a contrast.

Your partner writes a paragraph mentioning differences between polar climates, but emphasising their similarities: a comparison.

Then look at each other's paragraphs and notice the different ways you have written about the same facts.

12▶

9. Writing about your subject

Write several paragraphs comparing *or* contrasting two things/ideas associated with your own subject. Show the paragraphs to someone in the class. The person must make a table like the one completed in Exercise 1, showing similarities or differences.

Part III Additional exercises

10. Sentence combining

Join these sentences together to make a summary of Paragraph 3 of the passage on page 28.

(1) There is present interest in both polar regions.
(2) There is a fresh water shortage in the world.
(3) The world's population is using too much fresh water.
(4) 85% of the earth's fresh water is at the poles.
(5) The fresh water at the poles could solve the fresh water problem.
(6) A way of carrying polar ice needs to be found.

11. Completing a passage

When he first wrote the passage on page 28, the writer's second paragraph was longer. Here is how it continued. What do you think the missing words might be? (One word per space.)

It was one thing to . . . . . . the continent of Antarctica, and quite another to explore it. The name of Amundsen is . . . . . . in the exploration of

Antarctica. . . . . was he who first crossed the Arctic Ocean in 1903, and he was . . . . . . the first person to reach the South Pole. He . . . . . . Captain Scott there by 34 days. Scott, ... disappointed at having . . . . . . beaten by Amundsen, died while returning . . . . . . this expedition.

12. The Antarctic climate

Imagine you have to write an essay on the *Antarctic*. Use the information in Exercise 7 to write a paragraph about its climate. You can mention the Arctic climate as well, but your main interest is in the Antarctic.

Further reading

Fuchs V. and Hillary E. *The Crossing of Antarctica*, Penguin Books, 1960.
Kirwan L. P. *The White Road*, Hollis & Carter, 1959.
Brown R. N. R. *The Polar Regions*, Methuen, 1927.

Unit 7

Magic charms

Part I

1. Read this passage about magic* charms, then copy and complete the table below it.

A charm is a natural object which its owner thinks has some magic power. There are many kinds of charm. The Lhota Naga tribe* in Assam is an example of a tribe which believes that a certain type of stone* will bring good luck. Anyone who finds this stone will take it home with him. If he then has good luck, he will consider the stone a charm. For the Angami Naga tribe, on the other hand, any type of stone with a strange shape is a charm.

Plants as well as stones can be charms. The Guiana Indians have many plant charms, each one helping to catch a certain type of animal. The leaves of the plant usually look like the animal it is supposed to help to catch. Thus the charm for catching deer has a leaf which looks like deer horns*. Parts of dead animals, and even of people, can also become charms. The Tasmanians believed that a dead relative's bone would protect them from sickness and death, while the South Australian Buandik tribe believe that human hair prevents lightning* from striking!

There are various ways of making a charm more efficient, and the most common method is by heating. The Papuan Orokaiva tribe will make a 'charm mixture' to injure an enemy, and will then heat it by fire. As the heat increases, so will the enemy's discomfort. Another way is by inoculation*. When a hunter of the Tanala tribe (Malagasy Republic) wants to make his hunting successful, he cuts his lip* and puts a charm mixture in the cut. But there are stranger ways of making a charm efficient. If someone in the Zambian Ba-Ila tribe wants good luck, he can obtain a charm which only works if he commits incest*; and among the tribes of Gabun they believe a man must actually kill a near relative if certain charms are to work.

Types of charm	**Tribes who use them**
1. a certain type of stone	1. . . . .
2. any stone with a strange shape	2. . . . .
3.	3. Guiana Indians
4.	4. Tasmanians
5. human hair	5. . . . .
6. charm mixture (to injure enemy)	6. . . . .
7.	7. Tanala

2. Note-taking and summarising

Complete these notes on the passage. Then use them to write a short summary, mentioning the *main points* the writer makes. Do not include any examples in your summary.

A. **Types of charm**

(1) Stones (a) certain stones; (b) . . . . . .
(2) Plants
(3) . . . . . .

B. . . . .

(1) Heating
(2) . . . . . .
(3) Incest
(4) . . . . . .

3. Adding summarising sentences

(i) When we write, it often helps the reader if we include some sentences which summarise what we are about to say, or what we have just said, or both. Find sentences in the passage which do this.

(ii) Where would you put these summarising sentences in the passage? Would you have to change the passage in any way?

(a) Charms can also be plants, and parts of animal or human bodies.
(b) Charms, therefore, can be stones, plants, parts of animal or human bodies.
(c) In different tribes, stones, plants, parts of animal or human bodies are considered charms.
(d) This may be done by heating, inoculation, incest or murder.
(e) All these methods – heating, inoculation, incest or murder – can make charms more efficient.
(f) It is possible – by heating, inoculation, incest or murder – to make charms more efficient.

4. 'Even'

One use of the word 'even' is to *add something* to a point already made or suggested. A writer often uses it when he is telling us something *surprising*. For example:

> Parts of dead animals, and even people, can also be charms.

Here the writer is saying: 'As well as being parts of dead animals, charms can *also* be parts of dead people.' He thinks we will find this rather surprising.

Is the word 'even' being used correctly in these sentences from the passage?

line 4 (a) If he then has good luck, he will even consider the stone a charm.

line 11 (b) The Tasmanians believed that a dead relative's bone would protect them from sickness and even death.

line 16 (c) The Papuan Orokaiva tribe will even make a 'charm mixture' to injure an enemy.

line 21 (d) But there are even stranger ways of making a charm stronger.

***10*▶**

Part II Giving examples

5. Here is how the writer gives his example of a stone charm:

> The Lhota Naga tribe in Assam is an example of a tribe which believes that a certain type of stone will bring good luck.

Use the table you completed in Exercise 1 to give five more examples like this: '. . . . . . is/are an example of . . . . . . which . . . . . .'

6. The uses of charms

(i) Charms have many uses. Here are some examples taken from a passage describing the uses of charms. What do you think the *sentence before* each one might be?

(a) . . . . . . The Wataila of Kenya are a case* in point. They have charms which protect a person from lions*. Another example are the Creek Indians, who have charms against being injured.

(b) . . . . . . Tribes such as the Kurnai of Victoria use black stones as charms to kill their enemies. Similarly, the Akikuyo of Kenya have magic stones which will kill any evil* person who touches them.

(c) . . . . . . The Semang magicians are an example of this. Their magic stones will reveal* a person's illness, and help to cure* it. Indeed, the Baganda of Uganda have charms to cure almost every illness.

(d) . . . . . . Thus the Murngin of Canada use the blood of a dead man to make them good at hunting, while the Koniag of Alaska actually carry dead bodies in their boats when they go fishing.

(ii) Which expressions in these sentences show you that the writer is *giving examples*? Write them down.

***11*▶**

7. Taking care of charms

Most people who own charms take great care of them. Here is a passage about taking care of charms. Some examples are given below it. Rewrite the passage to include the examples. Use some of the expressions you wrote down in Exercise 6 (ii).

Because it is magical, good care must be taken of a charm in case it loses its power. The owner must be careful where he takes it (e.g. 1 and 2). He must also be careful who touches it (e.g. 3 and 4). Precautions* like this are easy to understand, but there are others which are quite strange (e.g. 5).

e.g. 1. Souk Indians – don't let charms touch ground.
e.g. 2. Singhalese – don't take charms to funerals.
e.g. 3. Wokonguru (Australia) – only owner can touch.
e.g. 4. Krita (Papua) – not even owner can touch.
e.g. 5. Ba-Ila (Zambia) – don't eat peas* when have a charm against rain. Sound of peas falling in pot is like thunder*. Sound like thunder might bring rain.

8. More uses of charms

Here are some more uses of charms. Write a paragraph about them.

1. Controlling the weather

e.g. 1. People on the D'Entrecasteaux Islands have an old pot which controls the weather. People must not look at pot, or there will be earthquake.
e.g. 2. Australia/New Guinea. Use pieces of wood as charms to bring rain.

2. Making invisible

e.g. Jukun tribe of N. Nigeria. They have charm to make them invisible. Leaves kept in the clothes of blind person.

3. Generally bringing good luck

e.g. 1. Fijian tribes keep fish's tooth.
e.g. 2. Omaha Indians have large shell.
e.g. 3. The stones of the Lhota Naga.

12▶

9. Writing about your subject

Write several paragraphs about something associated with your own subject. Give examples of some of the points you make. Show the paragraphs to someone in the class. They must make a table like the one completed in Exercise 1, showing *points* and *examples*.

Part III Additional exercises

10. Adding information

You want to add this information to lines 10–14 of the passage. Decide *where* you would put it, and *what words* you would use.

(a) The Bagobo of the Philippines use the foot of a dead bird as a charm.

(b) The dead relative's bone must come from his head.

(c) The human hair must be prepared in a certain way before it becomes a charm.

11. Completing a passage

Here is how the writer first wrote the passage on page 39. What do you think the missing words might be? (One word per space.)

Because it has magic power, a charm must be . . . . . . with great care in case it . . . . . . lose its power or . . . . . . cause damage*. There are often . . . . . . on where a charm should be taken, and who it may be touched . . . . Some of these precautions are . . . . . . understood, but others are in . . . . . . extremely strange.

12. Stone charms

Use the information given in the passage (page 36), Exercise 6 and Exercise 8 to write a paragraph on the use of *stones* as charms.

Further reading

Marwick M. *Witchcraft and Sorcery*, Penguin Books, 1970.
Mair L. *Witchcraft,* Weidenfeld and Nicolson, 1969.
Webster H. *Magic: A Sociological Study*, Stanford University Press, 1948.
Middleton J. *Magic, Witchcraft and Curing*, University of Texas Press, 1967.

Unit 8

Inventions

Part I

1. Read this passage about inventions, and complete the diagram. Write the words in your own books.

What are the causes that lead to* inventions* being made? Very often they are quite simply the result of nothing more than one individual's love of inventing things. Many of the inventions of the Greek inventor* Heron are, for example, just amusing toys. His machine for 'magically' opening temple* doors is a case in point. When a fire was lit on the altar* this made water in a large hollow* container turn to steam* and transfer through a tube* into a bucket*. When the bucket was full it would fall. Because the bucket was attached* to the temple doors by a system of ropes*, this would make the doors open. This 'amusing toy' was in fact a steam turbine*. In cases like this, the proverb that 'necessity is the mother of invention' is just not true.

Two factors are particularly important in the history of inventions. One is the part played by inspiration*, which can be far more vital than that of careful research. An example of this is the discovery of insulin* by Frederick Banting. He knew very little about the large amount of work which had been done in the field. But he succeeded where other more knowledgeable experimenters failed. The other factor is chance. Alexander Fleming's discovery of penicillin* was an accident. He was cultivating* bacteria*, when a cell* of what we now call penicillin fell on the bacteria. Fleming noticed how the cell began to destroy the bacteria, and this led him to his important discovery.

Because of the importance of inspiration and chance, it is very difficult to make accurate predictions about future inventions. The field of aviation gives us many examples of predictions that were wrong. In 1906 the '*Times*' newspaper said that all attempts to build an aeroplane would fail, and in 1910 the British Secretary of State for War said that aeroplanes would never be useful in wartime. Both predictions were of course very wrong.

2. Understanding the passage

Which of these sentences best summarises the writer's *main point*?

In Paragraph 1 the writer:

(a) describes the importance of the individual's love of invention.
(b) describes Heron's steam turbine.
(c) describes how some 'amusing toys' can be important inventions.

In Paragraph 2 the writer:

(a) describes the discovery of insulin and penicillin.
(b) considers the factors of inspiration and research in invention.
(c) considers the factors of inspiration and chance in invention.

How would you describe the *main point* the writer makes in Paragraph 3?

3. Vocabulary extension

Here are some expressions that could have been used in Paragraph 3, to make it a little more formal and academic. Decide where each expression could be used, and rewrite the paragraph. Use a dictionary if necessary.

(i) given
(ii) artificial* flight
(iii) provides
(iv) false
(v) claimed
(vi) doomed to
(vii) utility
(viii) proved to be

4. Putting two adjectives in front of a noun

(i) When two adjectives are put in front of a noun, we usually put the 'more important' one – one which perhaps describes something inherent* in the thing being described – next to the noun. If the adjectives are as 'important' as each other, the order does not matter. Find a noun in Paragraph 1 of the passage that has two adjectives in front of it. Can the order of adjectives be changed?

(ii) Imagine you want to add the underlined adjectives to the passage. Where would you put them?

line 3 (a) The Greek inventor Heron was famous.
line 9 (b) Heron's steam turbine was primitive*.
line 14 (c) The careful research is scientific research.
line 21 (d) Fleming's important discovery was a medical one.
line 23 (e) The future inventions are technological* ones.

10 ▶

Part II Types of descriptive statement (1)

Writing a description of any kind involves making many types of descriptive statement. In this Unit and the next we shall look at some of these types. The emphasis in this Unit is on describing objects.

5. When we mention something for the first time, we often use the *indefinite article* ('a', 'an'). But when we mention it again, we use the *definite article* ('the'). Here is an example from the passage:

> . . . *a* cell . . . fell on the bacteria. Fleming noticed how *the* cell . . .

Complete this description of the steam turbine by adding the words 'a' and 'the'.

Heron's steam turbine consists of . . . . . . large hollow container standing above . . . . . . fire. . . . . . . container is full of water. . . . . . . tube leads from . . . . . . container into . . . . . . bucket. . . . . . . bucket is attached to the doors by . . . . . . system of ropes.

6. Sentence combining

(i) The Greek Heron was famous for a number of inventions. Here is a diagram of his steam engine*, which like the steam turbine was used as a toy. Join the sentences below together to write a paragraph describing it.

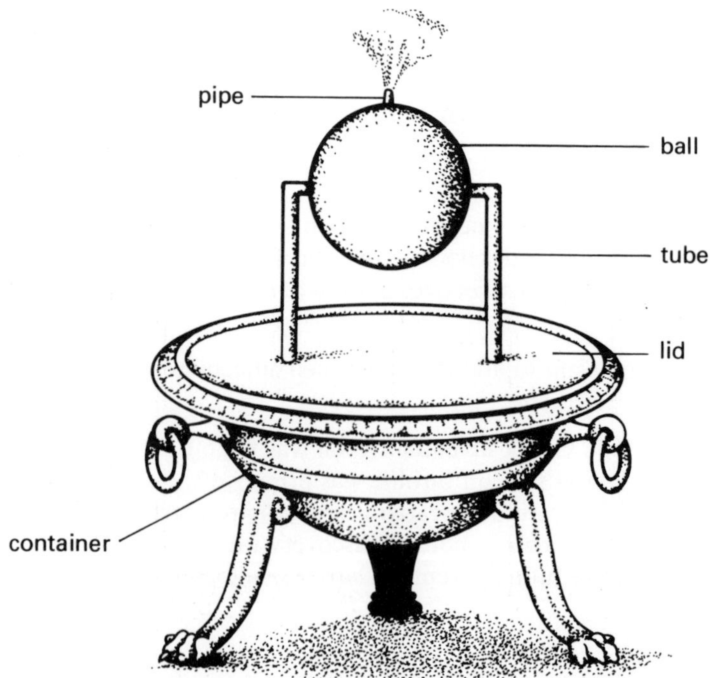

(1) Fire is lit under large container.
(2) Large container holds water.
(3) Large container is covered by lid.
(4) Two large tubes to from lid to ball.
(5) Ball is hollow.
(6) Ball is large.
(7) Two pipes come out of ball.
(8) Pipes are bent*.
(9) Pipes are small.
(10) Pipes bend in opposite directions.

(ii) How do you think the steam engine works? Add a sentence to your paragraph describing this.

11▶

7. The water clock

Here is a diagram of another of Heron's inventions – a water clock. Following the diagram is a description of the clock given by someone in a talk. Rewrite the description in a more formal, written style.

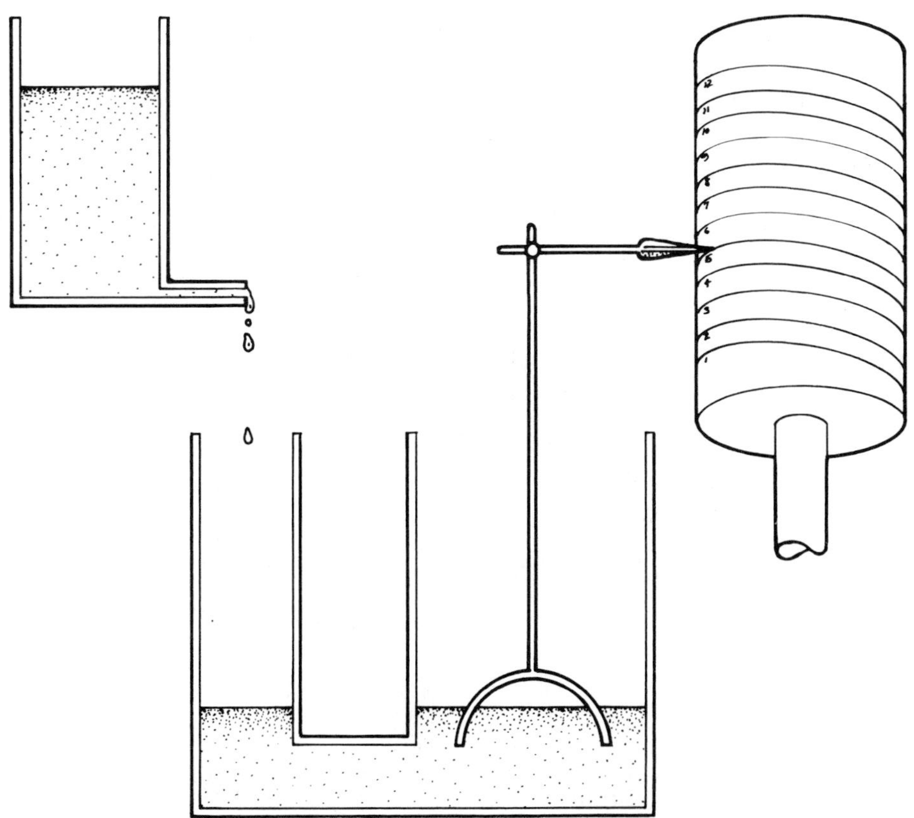

Well, it's really got three parts. There's a kind of tank* on the left which holds water. This tank has a very narrow opening, and the water drips* through this opening into the second container, also a kind of tank I suppose. Anyway, this second tank has got an object which floats* in it and the end of this is attached to a long pole* with an arrow* at the end. On the right there's a cylinder* with the numbers one to twelve written on it. It's very clever really. The water from the tank on the left drips into the tank in the middle. The level of the water gets higher, and so the floating thing rises. So the arrow moves up the cylinder. Heron put the numbers on the cylinder so that it takes an hour for the arrow to go from one number to the next. So you really have a twelve hour clock. Then after twelve hours, you just empty the tank in the middle and start all over again. Clever isn't it?

8. Ancient inventions

Many inventions were made in the Ancient World. Work in pairs. Student A looks at the diagram of an Egyptian invention on page 88. Student B looks at the diagram of a Greek machine, on page 58. Each write a description. Then show your description to your partner, who must try to draw a diagram of it. If his diagram is wrong, make your description clearer, so that the diagram is correct.

12 ▶

9. Writing about your subject

Write several paragraphs describing something associated with your own subject, but do not mention the name of the thing you are describing. Show your description to someone in the class (if possible someone studying the same subject). He must guess what you have described.

Part III Additional exercises

10. Summarising

Write a short summary of the passage on page 42. Mention *one example* of each point you make, but do not give too many details.

11. Reorganising a paragraph

The description of the steam turbine you completed in Exercise 5 began by saying something about the container. It described how the container was attached to the bucket, and how the bucket was attached to the doors: Container → Bucket → Doors.

Rewrite the description like this: Doors → Bucket → Container. Begin: 'The door is attached to a bucket . . .'

12. The Greek Heron

Use the information in the passage on page 42, in Exercise 6 and in Exercise 7 to write a paragraph about the Greek Heron and his inventions.

Further reading

Keller A. G. *A Theatre of Machines*, Chapman and Hall, 1964.
Hodges H. *Technology in the Ancient World*, Allen Lane, Penguin, 1970.
Pacey A. *The Maze of Ingenuity*, Allen Lane, Penguin, 1974.
Brumbaugh R. S. *Ancient Greek Gadgets and Machines*, Thomas Y. Crowell, 1966.

Unit 9

Sugar

Part I

1. Read this passage about sugar, and decide which paragraphs have these headings:

what sugar is	the advantages of sugar
sugar through the ages	present and future uses of sugar

Sugar is so much a part of our modern life that we only really think about it when, for some reason, we cannot obtain it. It has been known to man for at least 3,000 years, but has come into common use only in modern times. Until quite recently it was considered as a medicine and as a luxury for the very rich only.

Sugar is, then, very important to our civilisation. But what exactly is it? Of course, most of us recognise sugar immediately as the sweet material which we put in coffee or cakes. This common form of sugar is derived from* two plants: the sugar cane* (a type of grass which grows to a height of twenty feet) and the sugar beet* (which grows under ground). But there are in fact many types of sugar, and the chemist recognises hundreds of different varieties, each coming from a different source*.

About 90% of the sugar produced is used as food. Only 10% is used in industry for purposes other than food production. Yet sugar has great possibilities for use as the basis of chemicals. It can even be used for making plastics. In the future these potential uses will certainly be developed more than in the past.

There are many reasons why we should increase the production of sugar. Most important is that it is one of the most highly concentrated* of energy* foods. Thus sugar cane and beet produce an average of 7,000,000 calories* per acre*. In this way they have the advantage over potatoes which give only 4,000,000, while the figure for wheat* and beans* is 2,000,000 each. So three acres of land growing wheat, beans and potatoes give only slightly more 'energy' than one acre of sugar.

2. Note-taking and summarising

(i) In these notes on Paragraphs 2–4 of the passage, the writer uses several *signs* and *abbreviations*. Decide what they mean.

2. Common sugar → cane/beet
   100s diff. varieties.
3. 90% as food. 10% industry
   Poss. use – basis of chemicals & plastics.
4. We should increase sugar prod. ∵ concentrated.
   Sugar = 7 mill.c.p.a.
   Potatoes = 4 mill.; wheat/beans = 2 mill.
   ∴ 1 acre sugar almost same 'energy' as 3 acres potatoes, wheat, beans.

(ii) Use these notes to write a short summary of Paragraphs 2–4, making the same points that the writer makes.

3. Vocabulary extension

In Paragraph 3 the word 'use' (as a noun and verb) is repeated five times. Repeating the same word too often is not good style. With the help of a dictionary, rewrite the paragraph using the word less often.

4. Relative clauses*

In Exercise 4 of Unit 6 you saw how important it is to make the *main clause* of a sentence express the *main point*. Here is another example:

Sugar, which comes from* cane and beet, has been known for 3,000 years. In fact it has probably been used for longer.

The *main point* of the first sentence is that 'sugar has been known for 3,000 years'. The less important information (that sugar comes from cane and beet) is put in the relative clause.

(i)
(a) Sugar, which comes from cane and beet, has been known for 3,000 years.

(b) Sugar, which has been known for 3,000 years, comes from cane and beet.

The former is a grass, while the latter grows under ground.

Which sentence, (a) or (b), comes before the underlined sentence? Why? The answer is given at the bottom of page 50.

(ii) Decide whether (a) or (b) comes before each underlined sentence:

(a) Sugar, which is mainly used as a food, can also be the basis of chemicals.
(b) Sugar, which can be used as the basis of chemicals, is mainly used as a food.
In the future this use will be developed more.

(a) Wheat, which is used for making bread, gives 2,000,000 calories per acre.
(b) Wheat, which gives 2,000,000 calories per acre, is used for making bread.
This is fewer than potatoes give.

(a) Sugar, which is today in common use, was once used as a medicine.
(b) Sugar, which was once used as a medicine, is today in common use.
In fact we only think about it when we cannot obtain it.

(a) Calories, which give us energy, are highly concentrated in sugar.
(b) Calories, which are highly concentrated in sugar, give us energy.
It has many more calories than wheat.

Part II Types of descriptive statement (2)

5. Completing a passage

In the passage, the writer makes many types of descriptive statement. He tells us, for example, something about the *history* of sugar, its *uses*, the plant it is *derived from*, and its *advantages*.

Use expressions you saw in the passage to complete this paragraph. (One word per space.)

Sugar . . . . known to man for at least . . . . The common variety is . . . . . . from sugar cane and sugar . . . . , the former being a . . . . . . of grass which grows to a . . . . . . of 20 feet. Sugar is used primarily . . . . , though one . . . . . . use is as the basis . . . . One of the main advantages that sugar has . . . . . . other energy foods . . . . it is highly concentrated.

6. Parallel writing

Read this passage about Britain's most popular drink: tea. Then write one about cocoa*, to look as much like the tea passage as possible.

The reason why tea is so popular as a drink is that, unlike soft drinks for example, it contains a drug* which stimulates* the nervous system*. The tea plant is a kind of bush*, and tea is made from the very young leaves of this plant. Tea, used mainly as a drink but also as a kind of medicine, was first known to have been drunk in A.D. 780 in China, but was probably common long before that.

The answer is (b). The writer's *main points* are: Sugar comes from cane and beet. The former is a grass, while the latter grows under ground.

Cocoa

History: First brought to Europe by Columbus in 1502. (Prob. used by the Aztecs long before.)
Uses: Mainly as drink. Will be used more in future as filling* for cakes.
Derivation: From beans of cacao tree – bush found in most tropical regions.
Advantage: Gives more energy than coffee or tea (because contains a lot of fat*).

11▶

7. More about relative clauses . . .

Write sentences with relative clauses, to come before the underlined ones.

(a) [Cocoa comes from the cacao tree.]
[Cocoa gives more energy than coffee.]
This is a bush found in tropical regions.

(b) [Cocoa is used mainly as a drink.]
[Cocoa first came to Europe in 1502.]
Since then it has become very popular.

(c) [Tea stimulates the nervous system.]
[Tea can be used as a medicine.]
This is its main advantage over soft drinks.

(d) [Tea was first known to have been drunk in A.D. 780.]
[Tea is now a popular drink.]
In fact in Britain it is now the most popular drink.

8. . . . and more about tea

Tea has been the national drink of Britain for a long time. Here are some notes on tea. Use them to write a paragraph about the *history, uses, advantages* (and possible *disadvantages*) of tea. Before you write, decide how you are going to organise the paragraph.

17th C.	1st brought to Europe by Dutch*. 1st mentioned in England in 1658. Used 1st as medicine against sleepiness. All tea then China tea. 1st an aristocrat's* drink.
18th/19th C.	Drunk by all. But many thought it had disadvantages – bad for health. 1838 – 1st tea from India. 1878 – 1st tea from Ceylon.
20th C.	Average Englishman drinks 4 cups a day. Thought to calm and stimulate at same time.

12▶

9. Writing about your subject

In this Unit you have practised describing *history, uses, advantages* and *derivation.* Write several paragraphs associated with your own subject, describing some or all of these things. But do not mention *what* you are describing. Give your passage to someone in the class (if possible someone who is studying the same subject). The person must guess what you are describing.

Part III Additional exercises

10. Reorganising a paragraph

Rewrite the last paragraph of the passage on page 48 so that the *first* sentence is:

'Three acres of land growing wheat, beans and potatoes give only slightly more "energy" than one acre of sugar.'

Your *last* sentence should be:

'This is one of the many reasons why we should increase the production of sugar.'

11. Completing a passage

Here is how the writer first wrote the passage on page 50. What do you think the missing words might be? (One word per space.)

One reason for the . . . . . . of tea is that, unlike soft drinks, it contains a drug . . . . . . stimulating the nervous system. Tea, derived . . . . . . the leaves of the tea plant, has been used since . . . . . . times. . . . . it was first known to have been drunk in A.D. 780 in China. It was possibly used long before that, ... mainly as a drink, it is also considered . . . . . . a kind of medicine.

12. Tea and cocoa

Use the information given in Exercise 6 to write a passage *comparing* and *contrasting* cocoa and tea.

Further reading

Pyke M. *Technological Eating*, John Murray, 1972.
van Hook A. *Sugar*, The Ronald Press Company, 1949.
Harler C. R. *Tea Manufacture*, Oxford University Press, 1963.
Chatt E. M. *Cocoa*, Interscience Inc., 1953.

Unit 10 (Consolidation Unit)

The dangers of space* travel

Part I

1. Read the first paragraph of this passage, *covering the rest of it with a piece of paper*. What do you think the writer is going to talk about next? Discuss in class. Read each paragraph in the same way, and discuss the same question.

Not so long ago it was assumed that the dangers man would meet in space would be terrible, the main ones being radiation* and the danger of being hit by meteors*. It is perhaps worth remembering that less than two centuries ago, the dangers of train travel seemed similarly terrible. A man would certainly die, it was thought, if carried along at a speed of 30 m.p.h.

There are two sorts of radiation man must fear in space. The first is radiation from the sun, and this is particularly dangerous when the sun is very active and explosions are occurring on its surface. The second, less harmful form comes from the so-called Van Allen Belts. These are two areas of radiation about 1,500 miles away from the earth. Neither of these forms of radiation are a danger to us on the earth, since we are protected by our atmosphere. Specifically, it is that part of our atmosphere known as the ozonosphere which protects us. This is a belt of the chemical ozone* between 12 and 21 miles from the ground which absorbs all the radiation.

Once outside the atmosphere, however, man is no longer protected, and radiation can be harmful in a number of ways. A distinction must be drawn between the short-* and long-term* effects of radiation. The former are merely unpleasant, but just because an astronaut* returning from a journey in space does not seem to have been greatly harmed, we cannot assume that he is safe. The long-term effects can be extremely serious, even leading to death.

One solution to the dangers of radiation is to protect the spaceship* by putting some kind of shield* around it. This was in fact done on the Apollo spaceships which landed on the moon. But this solution is not possible for longer journeys – to Mars for example – because the shield would need to be very large, and could not be carried. Another solution, not in fact possible at present, would be to surround the spaceship with a magnetic field* to deflect* the radiation. In all, we have to conclude that there is at present no complete solution to the problem of radiation.

2. Note-taking

(i) Complete these notes on the passage:

Dangers of space travel (i) . . . .
(ii) . . . .

Types of radiation (i) . . . .
(ii) . . . .

Effects of radiation (i) . . . .
(ii) . . . .
Solutions (i) . . . .
(ii) . . . .

(ii) The passage is taken from a longer one about the dangers of space travel. How do you think it continues? You will find the answer later in this Unit.

3. Revision

(i) In Unit 6 you practised writing *contrasts* and *comparisons* using 'whereas' and 'both'. Does the writer of the passage *compare* or *contrast* the things below? Decide, then compare or contrast using 'whereas' or 'both'.

(a) man's fears of the dangers of train and space travel
(b) the effects of radiation from the sun and from Van Allen Belts
(c) the dangers of radiation inside and outside the earth's atmosphere
(d) the long- and short-term effects of radiation
(e) the possibility of using a shield on long and short space journeys

(ii) In Units 6 and 9 you saw that the *main clause* of a sentence expresses the *main point*. Decide which of these sentences best describe what the writer is saying in the passage.

(a) Although we are protected from radiation on the earth, astronauts who leave the earth are in danger from it.
(b) Although astronauts who leave the earth are in danger from radiation, we are protected from it on the earth.

(a) Although the short-term effects of radiation are small, the long-term effects can be serious.
(b) Although the long-term effects of radiation can be serious, the short-term effects are small.

(a) Although there is no complete solution to the problem of radiation, a shield can protect spaceships on short journeys.
(b) Although a shield can protect spaceships on short journeys, there is no complete solution to the problem of radiation.

4. Meteors

In the passage the writer describes *types* of radiation, *effects* of radiation, and *solutions* to the problem, in that order. The passage continues with a description of the danger of being hit by meteors. Use these notes to write a paragraph on this danger. It should have the same structure: types → effects → solutions.

Meteors

(a) Groups. Move round the sun. Earth passes through groups of meteors several times a year. Most spectacular are the August Perseids.
(b) Individual. Meteors coming from any direction at any time.

Avoidance

Groups can be avoided because they are predictable.
Shield can protect against individual meteors. But same problem of weight.

Danger

Large meteor could destroy spaceship.
Small meteor could come into spaceship and depressurise* it.
Danger is small (though Russians say 2 of their spaceships hit by meteors).

Part II Organising a description

The way we *organise our descriptions* depends on exactly what we want to say. Here are two points which the writer makes in the passage:
(1) We are protected from radiation on the earth.
(2) Astronauts who leave the earth are in danger from radiation.
Because the passage is about space travel, Point (2) is the writer's *main point*. Notice that he puts this *main point* second. When making two points like this, writers often put their main point second.

5. Imagine you are writing a passage describing how the earth is protected from radiation. You want to make Points (1) and (2) above, but your *main point* is Point (1). Write a short paragraph, making the main point second.

6. Food on space journeys

If man is to go on long space journeys, food will be a big problem. One possible solution is for astronauts to eat algae. Here is some information about algae:

They taste horrible.
They are easy to grow. All they really need is sunlight.
They are very rich in protein*.
Algae are small green sea plants.
An astronaut would certainly get very unhappy if he had to eat algae for a long time.
They look horrible.

Work in pairs. One of you writes a paragraph with Point (1) below as the main point; the other with Point (2) as the main point. Then compare your paragraphs.

(1) Although algae have certain disadvantages, they can be used as food for astronauts.
(2) Although algae can be used as food for astronauts, they have certain disadvantages.

7. The problem of acceleration* and deceleration*

We usually speak in a far less organised way than we write. Here is what one lecturer, talking informally to some students, says about another problem of space travel – what happens when spaceships accelerate* and decelerate* quickly:

It certainly is a problem, and the Americans have made a machine called a 'human centrifuge'* to do tests with. It's a kind of long pole with a seat on the end. The astronaut sits on the seat, and the seat turns round at great speed. They use it to study the problem. Pilots of very fast planes are always complaining about this. They can actually lose consciousness* if they accelerate or decelerate too quickly. Actually, strange as it may seem, acceleration and deceleration have exactly the same effect – it's the same problem. The important thing is that the astronaut should be facing the direction he is travelling in. So when he leaves the earth he should be facing upwards, and when he returns to the earth he should be pointing downwards. The experiments with the 'human centrifuge' show this. The effect is worst when the astronaut is facing the direction opposite to the one he is travelling in.

Write a paragraph about acceleration and deceleration for a passage on the dangers of space travel. First plan the paragraph; then, when you write it, make sure the style is for written (not spoken) English.

8. Writing about your subject

In Unit 6 you practised *comparing* and *contrasting*; and in Unit 9 you described *history, uses, advantages* and *derivation*. Write several paragraphs comparing and contrasting two ideas or objects associated with your own subject. Mention some of the things you practised describing in Unit 9.

Further reading

Moore P. *Space in the Sixties*, Penguin Books, 1963.
O'Neil G. K. *The High Frontier*, Cape, 1977.
Glasstone S. *Sourcebook on the Space Sciences*, Van Nostrand Co. Inc., 1965.

Diagram referring to Unit 8, Exercise 8

The Greek machine for squeezing oil from olives

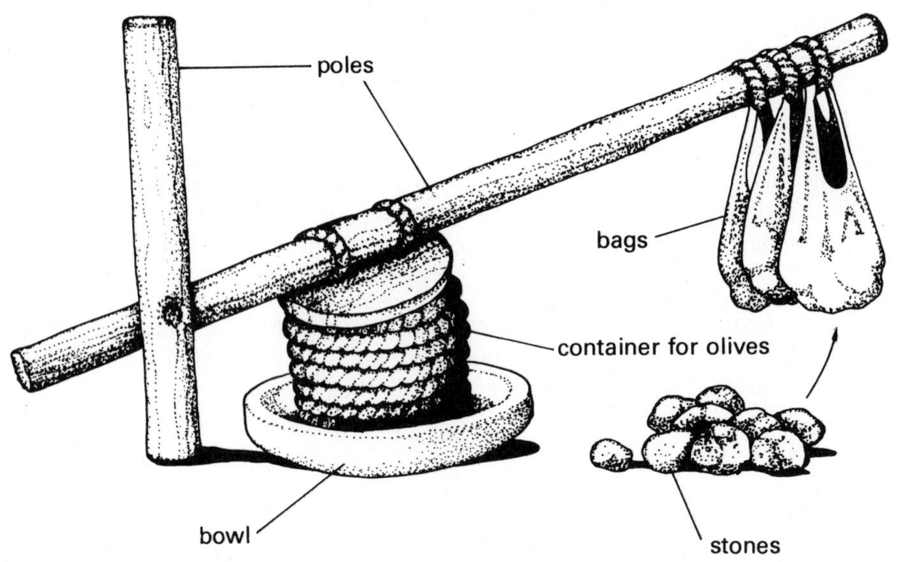

Words:	long	thin	sharp end
	conical	at one end	winding round

Part 2

Describing processes and events

Unit 11

Conditioning

Part I

1. In this passage about conditioning, the writer describes, several experiments*. Read the passage, then copy and complete the table which follows it to show the experimenters'* *aims* and *how* they reached them.

When animals (including man) eat it is normal for the mouth to water. This is called salivation. It is a natural reflex*, and was studied by the Russian physiologist* Pavlov whose famous experiments on the salivation of dogs are important in the history of modern psychology.

Though salivation is natural, Pavlov noticed that a dog would salivate not just when it was eating, but also when it saw the man who usually fed it. In Pavlov's early experiments he simply showed the dog some bread, which he then allowed it to eat. After a while the sight of the experimenter was enough to make the dog salivate. We cannot call this a natural reflex because a dog does not normally salivate at the sight of man. It is what psychologists call a 'conditioned response'. The dog has been taught, or 'conditioned'*, to salivate when he sees the man.

Having decided to study this, Pavlov developed scientific methods for doing so. In order to make sure the experimenter did not disturb the dog, dog and experimenter were put in separate rooms. Pavlov even put the dog in a kind of frame* to make it stand still. He invented a system of tubes for giving the dog food, and watched what happened from outside the room. He found that he could condition the dog to salivate at almost any event – when a bell rang or a light flashed*, for example – as long as this event was followed by food.

The American psychologist Skinner developed this idea of conditioning. He found he could condition animals to do quite complicated things by using a technique* he called 'shaping'*. He could teach pigeons, for example, to play table tennis. At first he gave them a reward for knocking the ball a short distance in the right direction. Slowly he increased the distance they must knock the ball before getting the reward, and eventually they received it only when they knocked the ball past their 'opponent'.

Aims	How
1. make sure experimenter did not disturb dog	1. put dog and experimenter in separate rooms
2. make dog stand still	2. . . . .
3.	3. invented a system of tubes
4. make dog salivate at almost any event	4. . . . .
5.	5. shaping
6. teach pigeons to knock ball in right direction	6. . . . .

2. Describing a sequence

In what order do these things happen? Decide, then use the notes to write a short passage describing the sequence of events in *Pavlov's experiment*.

Pavlov's experiment

(a) Rang a bell.
(b) Gave dog food.
(c) Dog salivated.
(d) Put dog in room alone.
(e) Put dog in frame.

Skinner's experiment

(a) Gave pigeons reward for knocking ball past opponent.
(b) Gave pigeons reward for knocking ball in right direction.
(c) Increased distance pigeons must knock ball.

3. Adding information

You want to add these words to Paragraph 4 of the passage. Decide *where* you would put them.

(a) In this way their behaviour is conditioned by a process of shaping.
(b) . . . . . . which they would not normally do.
(c) Many of his experiments were with pigeons.
(d) . . . . . . and even applied it to man.
(e) . . . . . . hitting it with their beaks*.

4. The passive

(i) The passive is quite common in formal writing. If it is important to mention who 'performed' the action, a phrase beginning with the word 'by' follows the passive verb. If it is not important, we leave this out. Look at Paragraphs 1 and 2. Find a passive with 'by', and one without. Why has the writer mentioned who performed the action in one case, and not in the other?

(ii) Change these verbs into the passive. Decide whether you need a 'by' phrase or not.
line 7 (a) showed
line 9 (b) call
line 18 (c) condition
line 21 (d) developed
line 26 (e) received

10►

Part II Expressing purpose and means

5. In order to make sure the experimenter did not disturb the dog, dog and experimenter were put in separate rooms.

In this sentence, the writer expresses what Pavlov aimed to do (PURPOSE), and how he did it (MEANS). Use the table you completed in Exercise 1 to make five more sentences like this.

6. Completing a passage

Here is another way of expressing MEANS:

He found he could condition animals to do quite complicated things by using a technique he called 'shaping'.

This passage about Pavlov's experiments contains more examples like this. Try to complete it. (More than one word goes in each space.)

By using a technique called conditioning, Pavlov . . . . He developed scientific methods for doing this. He made sure that the experimenter did not disturb the dog, by . . . . Then, by . . . . . . , he made the dog stand still. Pavlov next rang a bell, and he found that the dog would salivate. By using a system of tubes, he then . . . .

11►

7. Eating fire

Most of us do not salivate when fire comes close to our face. The 'fire-eater' you see at a circus* is not burned because he has learned to salivate with fire in his mouth. His saliva* protects him. We can condition ourselves to salivate close to fire by a process of shaping. Here is how:

- Light a match and hold it near your face. Do this several times until you continue to salivate normally. (*Do not let the match touch the outside of your mouth, where there is no saliva!*)
- Move an unlighted match quickly in and out of your mouth. Continue until you can do so without your saliva drying.
- Move a lighted match quickly in and out of your mouth. Continue until you can salivate normally.
- Leave the match in your mouth for two or three seconds.
- Close your mouth quickly over the match.
- When you can put a flame in your mouth like this, you should also be able to put a match out against your tongue . . . if you are salivating!

When describing an experiment in a formal way, we do not usually use the possessive pronouns and adjectives – I/my, you/your. We can often avoid the pronouns by using the passive without a 'by' phrase. The adjectives can be avoided when talking about a part of the body, by using 'the'. Find an example of this use of 'the' in the passage.

Write a formal description of the 'fire-eating experiment'. Do not use the words 'you' and 'your'. Begin: 'A match is first lit and held . . .'

8. Adding an opening paragraph

Descriptions of experiments often begin with a paragraph saying what the PURPOSE of the experiment is, and *how* it was done (MEANS). Add a short opening paragraph like this to the passage you wrote in Exercise 7.

9. Writing about your subject

Every subject is concerned with *how* things are done, and *why* they are done. Write an essay on something associated with your own subject. Describe PURPOSES and MEANS. Show the essay to someone in the class. They must make a table like the one completed in Exercise 1, showing *aims* and *how*.

Part III Additional exercises

10. Reorganising a paragraph

Here are some notes on Paragraph 1. Rewrite the paragraph so that the points are made in this order: Salivation a natural reflex. Salivation = mouth watering when animals eat. Also man. Studied by Russian Pavlov. Experiments on dogs. Pavlov a physiologist. Experiments important to history of modern psychology.

11. The teaching machine

Skinner also experimented with shaping human behaviour, and for this he invented a 'teaching machine'. This machine can be used for teaching many different subjects. Look at the diagram and the description of what happens. Can you see how the machine works?

(a) Student is given information and asked a question (higher window)
(b) Student writes his answer (lower window)
(c) Student turns wheel
(d) Student checks answer (appears in lower window)

Now complete these sentences about the teaching machine:

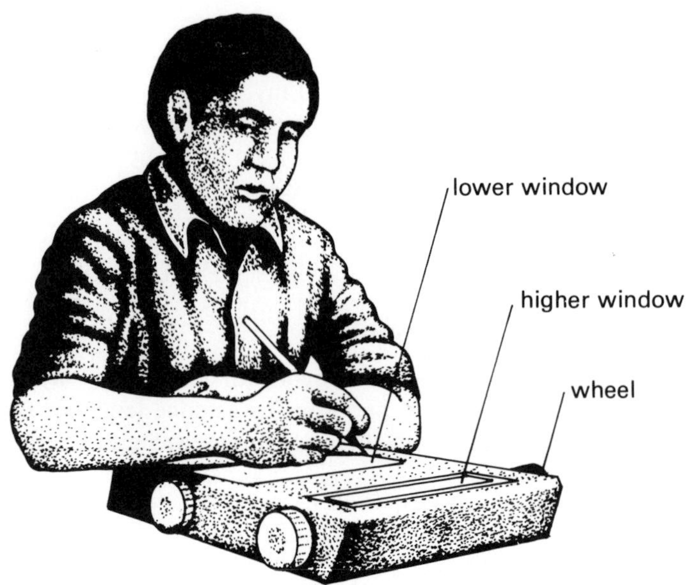

(a) Skinner shaped* human behaviour by means of . . . . . .
(b) The higher window is for . . . . . .
(c) The lower window has a space for . . . . . .
(d) The student answers the question by . . . . . .
(e) The student turns the wheel in order to . . . . . .

12. Write a passage describing the teaching machine and saying how it works.

Further reading

Walker S. *Learning and Reinforcement,* Methuen, 1975.

Kay H., Dodd B. and Sime M. *Teaching Machines and Programmed Instruction*, Penguin Books, 1968.

Barlow J. A. *Stimulus and Response*, Harper and Row, 1968.

Unit 12

The biological clock

Part I

1. Understanding the passage

Read this passage about the biological* clock. Which of the statements following the passage does the writer make?

It was long ago noticed that different plants open and close at different times of the day. In fact, in the nineteenth century they used to make gardens in the shape of a clock face, with different flowers opening at different times. It was possible to tell the time just by looking at this 'flower clock'. No one really understands why flowers open and close like this at particular times, but recently some interesting experiments have been done. In one, flowers were put in a laboratory in constant darkness. One might predict that these flowers, not having any information about the time of day, would not open as they usually do. But in fact they continue to open as if they were in a normal garden. This suggests that they have some mysterious way of keeping time; that they have, in other words, a kind of 'biological clock'.

It has recently been found that not just flowers, but all living things (including man) have 'cycles* of activity'. Because these cycles last about twenty-four hours, they are called 'circadian cycles' (circa = about, diem = day). Some scientists believe these cycles are controlled by an 'internal* clock'. According to this theory, the flowers in the laboratory open because their 'internal clock' tells them to do so.

There are other scientists, including the American Dr Brown, who believe that the biological clock is controlled by the environment. He studied the way oysters* open and close their shells at high and low tide*. He took some oysters from the sea to his laboratory a thousand miles away in Illinois. According to the 'internal clock' theory one would expect the oysters to open and close as they had done before. But in fact their cycle changed. Brown and his colleagues could not understand this until they asked themselves the question: 'If Illinois were on the sea, when would high and low tides take place?' He found that the oysters were opening and closing at exactly these times. Brown concluded that the oysters' cycle was controlled by changes in the atmosphere – changes that, in places where there is a sea, are associated with the tides.

Paragraph 1

(a) Because of recent experiments, we now understand why flowers open and close at particular times.

(b) Recent experiments suggest flowers have a kind of biological clock.

Paragraph 2

(a) Flowers and a few other living things have 'cycles of activity'.
(b) All scientists now believe circadian cycles are controlled by an 'internal clock'.

Paragraph 3

(a) Dr Brown's laboratory is by the sea.
(b) The oysters in Dr Brown's laboratory did not open and close as before.

2. Sentence combining

Join the sentences together to make a paragraph.

(1) Flowers in darkness open and close as normal.
(2) Flowers have a kind of 'biological clock'.
(3) Some scientists believe the clock is internal.
(4) Some scientists do not believe the clock is internal.
(5) Dr Brown does not believe the clock is internal.
(6) Dr Brown's experiments on oysters make him doubt* the clock is internal.
(7) Dr Brown's experiments on oysters were done in Illinois.

3. Clarifying a point

If we wish to *clarify* something we have said, we can say it in another way, using the expression 'in other words'. Find an example of this expression in the passage. Notice where in the sentence the expression is put.

Which points in the passage are the following clarifying? Where would you put them in the passage? Where would you write 'in other words'?

(a) They are given no light at all.
(b) The environment* is unimportant.
(c) Their circadian cycle should continue unchanged.
(d) He changed their environment completely.

4. Vocabulary extension

Here are some expressions that could have been used in lines 7–11 to make them a little more formal and academic. Decide where each expression could be used. Use a dictionary if necessary.

(i) deprived* of
(ii) do maintain their normal cycles
(iii) leads to the hypothesis*
(iv) means
(v) possess
(vi) what might be called

5. Making a predicate* longer

In written and spoken English we often try to make the predicate of a sentence longer and more complicated than the subject. We particularly try to avoid ending a sentence with the main verb. For example, instead of saying or writing 'he's swimming', we might prefer 'he's having a swim'.

Rewrite the underlined sentences below so that the predicates are longer.

(a) Different plants open and close at different times. Most plants do.
(b) One might predict these flowers would not open. They did.
(c) It is not just flowers which have 'cycles of activity'. All living things do.
(d) Some scientists do not believe the 'internal clock' theory. Dr Brown does not.
(e) One would expect the oysters to open and close as before. But their cycle changed.

Part II Expressing prediction and expectancy

6. When describing a process, we sometimes wish to say not only what happens, but also what we *predicted* would happen. Here are two sentences from the passage which do this:

> A. One might predict that these flowers would not open as they usually do.
> B. One would expect the oysters to open and close as they had done before.

Change sentence A so that it uses 'expect . . . to' and sentence B so that it uses 'predict that . . .'

7. Circadian cycles in man

One way of studying circadian cycles in people is to put them in a cave*, so that they have no contact* with the outside world. In the left-hand column of the table below are notes about some things that the 'internal clock' theory predicts would happen if you did this. Make sentences using 'predict' and 'expect.'

	Prediction	**Reality**
1.	People able to judge time	Could no longer judge time
2.	People sleep and wake at same times	Cycles of sleeping and waking very irregular
3.	'Cycle of activity' remains as before	'Cycle of activity' becomes longer than 24 hours
4.	People eat as usual	Eat more often than usual
5.	People's toilet habits remain the same	Toilet habits change

8. Contrasting prediction and reality

> According to the 'internal clock' theory the oysters should have opened and closed as before. In fact the cycle changed.

In these sentences the writer contrasts a prediction (what *should have* happened) with reality (what *in fact* happened).

(i) Use the table in Exercise 7 to make more sentences contrasting prediction and reality.

(ii) Write a paragraph contrasting what the internal clock theory predicts would happen to people in caves, and what in fact happened.

13 ▶

9. 'Morning' and 'evening' types

Some people are more active in the mornings, while others feel and work better in the evenings. Nearly all of us feel particularly tired every six to eight hours, usually at 4.00, 12.00, 18.00 and 24.00.

The following two graphs predict how a 'morning' and an 'evening' type will do an experimental task* at different times of the day. Imagine you are going to do (*but have not yet done*) an experiment on Mr X and Mr Y. Use the table to write a paragraph predicting what will happen.

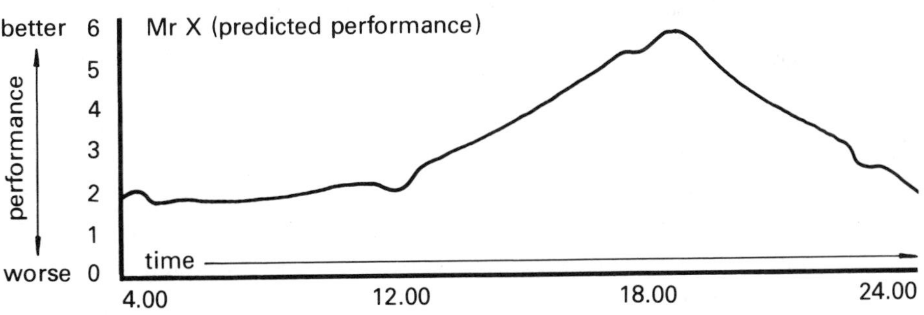

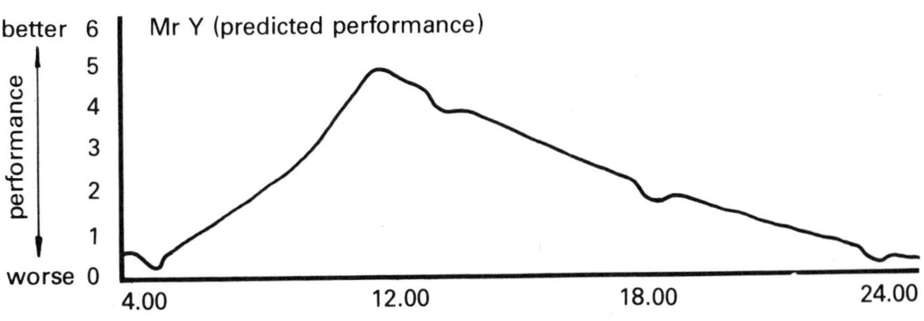

According to the graphs Mr X is (a morning / an evening) type and it is therefore . . . . . . that he will perform the task (better / worse) at 19.00 than at 11.00. Mr Y (on the other hand / also) is (predicted / expected) to give his (best / worst) performance at 11.00. Both men (should have performed / should perform) least efficiently at (4.00 / 24.00) and if the graphs are correct both (should feel / should have felt) short periods of particular . . . . . . at six to eight hour intervals. This (should have reflected / should reflect*) in their ability to perform the task. We (expect / predict) Mr X's overall performance to be (better / worse) than Mr Y's.

10. Mr X's and Mr Y's actual performance

Sometimes the best predictions go wrong! Here is how Mr X and Mr Y actually did the task. Write part of your report on the experiment. Contrast *prediction* and *reality*.

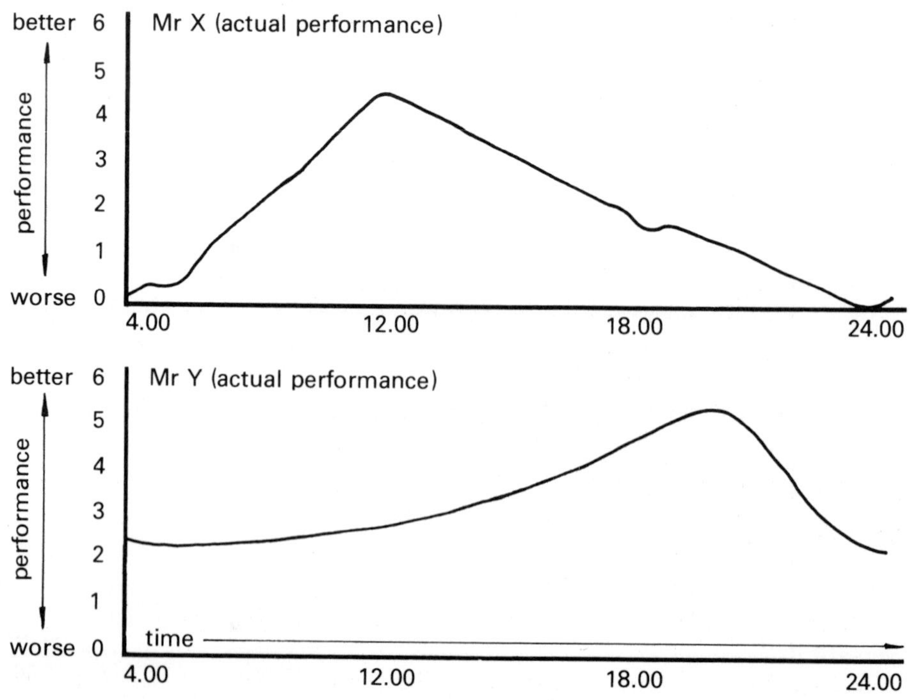

14▶

11. Writing about your subject

Before doing an experiment or beginning any kind of study, you usually have an idea of what you expect to find. Think of an experiment or study associated with your own subject, and write an essay expressing your predictions.

Part III Additional exercises

12. Completing a passage

Here is how the writer first began the passage on page 66. What do you think the missing words might be? (One word in each space.)

Different plants open and close at different times, ... it is not known why. . . . . . . was noticed long ago, ... recently some interesting experiments have been done. In the nineteenth century they used to make '. . . . .'. These were gardens in the shape of a clock face. . . . . . . at this face it was possible to tell the time, ... the flowers opened at different times. Flowers . . . . . . continue to open at particular times when they are kept in constant darkness, ... that they have some mysterious biological clock.

13. The internal clock theory

According to the internal clock theory, living things are born with internal clocks which work in any environment. How can we decide if the theory is right? Here are some things we can expect if this theory is correct. Write a short passage expressing these predictions.

All members of the species should have the clock.
It should be present in the living thing from birth.
The clock should work in any environment.
The clock should work in any temperature.
The clock should not be affected by any drug* given to the living thing.

14. In the passage on page 66, the writer talks about circadian cycles in flowers and oysters. Use the information given in Exercise 7 and Exercise 9 to add a short paragraph about circadian cycles in man.

Further reading

Luce G. G. *Body Time*, Temple Smith, 1972.
Brown F. A., Hastings J. W. and Palmer J. D. *The Biological Clock: two views*, Academic Press, 1970.
Bünning E. *The Physiological Clock*, English Universities Press, 1973.

Unit 13

Words

Part I

1. In this passage, the writer discusses several reasons why words change their meanings. Read the passage, then copy and complete the table which follows it.

Why do words change their meanings? Sometimes this happens because of a linguistic association. The word 'constitutional' for example is an adjective meaning, roughly, 'for health'. It was long used in the phrase 'a constitutional walk', which was a walk taken for reasons of health. The phrase became so common that the word 'walk' was forgotten, and today a walk taken for health reasons is thus known simply as 'a constitutional'.

Changes in meaning also happen when the thing a word describes changes form. The word 'car', from Latin 'carrus', is an example. It originally meant a 'four-wheeled coach'*. The modern car is not at all like the old four-wheeled coach. The thing has changed, so the word has changed meaning with it.

Meaning change can also take place through a desire to avoid talking about an unpleasant subject. The word 'undertaker' is an example of this. It originally meant 'someone who undertakes* to make special arrangements'. Our modern travel agent might once have been called a 'travel undertaker'. One expression using the word was 'funeral undertaker'. The word 'funeral' was dropped*, however, because it reminded people of the unpleasant subject of death. The result is that today 'undertaker' has lost its general sense, and now means 'the man who arranges funerals'.

The words 'limbs'* and 'waist' were used in strange ways by nineteenth century American ladies. This was caused by their desire to avoid talking about impolite subjects. The words 'legs' and 'body' were, they felt, rude. Consequently they talked about 'piano limbs' instead of 'piano legs' and spoke of their own 'waists', to avoid using the word 'body'.

A change in meaning is often made necessary by a scientific discovery. When the scientist Kepler needed a word to describe a small planet going round a larger one, he took the word 'satellite' which really means an 'attendant'* or 'life guard'*. Today the word has many meanings and is used for example in the field of politics . . .

Reason	Example
1. linguistic association	1. 'constitutional'
2.	2. . . . .
3.	3. . . . .
4. Desire to avoid talking about impolite subjects.	4. . . . .
5.	5. . . . .

2. Adding information

Here are some comments on Paragraph 5. Rewrite the paragraph to include these points:

(a) Kepler was a 17th century astronomer.
(b) A satellite is not always a planet. It can be any 'heavenly body'*.
(c) 'Satellite' comes from the Latin 'satellitis'.
(d) Show the association between the meaning of 'satellite' in politics and its meaning in astronomy.

3. Paragraph and sentence topic

(i) In a *paragraph*, the *main topic* is often mentioned in the first sentence. Find examples of this in the passage. How could you rewrite the beginning of Paragraph 4 so that the *main topic* is mentioned in the first sentence?

(ii) In a *sentence*, the *main topic* is often mentioned in the first few words. Rewrite the opening sentences of Paragraphs 2, 3 and 5 so that the main topics of *sentence* and *paragraph* are mentioned in the first few words. Begin:
Paragraph 2: When the thing . . .
Paragraph 3: A desire to avoid . . .
Paragraph 5: A scientific discovery . . .

4. Parallel writing

The writer's example in Paragraph 2 is the word 'car'. An example of a similar meaning change is the word 'paper'. Rewrite the paragraph using 'paper' rather than 'car' as the example:

'Paper' from Egyptian 'papyrus' = grass originally used for paper. Modern paper unlike 'papyrus'.

10 ▶

Part II Expressing cause, effect, reason and result

5.

(i) Here is one way of expressing *cause* or *reason*:

> This was caused by their desire to avoid talking about impolite subjects.

Use the table you completed in Exercise 1 to express *cause* or *reason* with 'caused by'.

(ii) The sentences in (i) begin with the word 'this'. What does 'this' refer back to each time? What sentences could come *just before* the ones in (i)?

6.

(i) In the passage the writer uses different ways of expressing *cause, reason, effect* and *result.* Find examples of these.

(ii) How would you complete these sentences?

(a) The word 'undertaker' changed meaning because of . . . . . .
(b) The phrase 'a constitutional walk' became very common. Consequently . . . . . .
(c) Kepler needed a word to describe a small planet going round a larger one; so . . . . . .
(d) The word 'car' changed meaning through . . . . . .
(e) They felt 'legs' and 'body' were rude words. Thus . . . . . .
(f) The word 'walk' was forgotten. The result was that . . . . . .

7. Cockney rhyming slang

Cockneys are working people born in London. They have a special way of talking, called 'rhyming slang'. For example, instead of saying 'feet' they use the expression 'plates of meat', simply because 'feet' and 'meat' rhyme*.

(i) Here are some notes taken from a passage on Cockney rhyming slang. The two signs ∴ (expressing *effect, results*) and ∵ (expressing *cause, reason*) have been left out. Decide when each is used.

People in the same social class working together often like to separate themselves from society. . . . . . . develop secret languages, e.g. Cockney rhyming slang. Begun in 19th C. By 1914 all Cockneys using it . . . . . . found it amusing. Cockneys are Londoners . . . . . . many slang expressions associated with London, e.g. expression for 'arm' = 'Chalk Farm' (name of part of London). Often difficult for non-Cockney to understand slang . . . . . . last part of rhyme gets dropped, e.g. expression for 'head' was 'loaf of bread'. Abbreviated to 'loaf'*. . . . . . . today 'loaf' = 'head'. . . . . . . if Cockney says 'use your loaf' = 'use your head' (i.e. 'think'!).

(ii) Use these notes to write a passage about Cockney rhyming slang. Use some of the expressions you saw in Exercise 6(ii).

11▶

8. English as a world language

Professor X is an expert* on the English Language. He thinks that one day English will become the world language. In this interview Professor X explains why he thinks this will be the case:

Q: Why do you think English will become the world language?
A: Well, for one thing*, it's so commonly used. The only language which is used by more people is Chinese.
Q: Why is English spoken by so many people?
A: It's spoken in many countries of the world because of the British Empire. And now of course there's the influence of America as well.
Q: Many students find English a difficult language to learn . . .
A: Oh, all languages are difficult to learn! But English does have two great advantages.
Q: What are they?
A: Well, first of all it has a very international vocabulary. It has many German, Dutch, French, Spanish and Italian words in it. So speakers of those languages will find many familiar words in English. Also, English has words from many other languages as well.
Q: Why is that?
A: Well, partly because English speakers have travelled a lot. They bring back words with them. So English really does have an international vocabulary.
Q: And what's the other advantage of English?
A: It's that English grammar is really quite easy. For example, it doesn't have dozens of* different 'endings'* (or 'suffixes' as we call them) for its nouns, adjectives and verbs. Not like Latin, Russian and German for example.
Q: Why is that?
A: Well, it's quite interesting actually. It's because of the French! When the French ruled England, French was the official language and only the common* people spoke English. They tried to make the language as simple as possible, so they made the grammar easier . . .

Later Professor X writes an article called 'English as the World Language'. Write part of this article, making the points mentioned in the interview. The article must be written quite formally.

12▶

9. Writing about your subject

Write an essay on something associated with your own subject. Describe *causes, effects, reasons* and *results*. Show the essay to someone in the class. He must make a table like the one completed in Exercise 1, showing *causes, effects, reasons* and *results*.

Part III Additional exercises

10. Reorganising a paragraph

Rewrite Paragraph 1 of the passage on page 72, making the points in this order:

Why do words change meanings? Sometimes linguistic association. e.g. today 'a constitutional' = 'walk taken for health reasons'. Originally 'a constitutional walk' (adj. 'constitutional' = 'for health'). Phrase so common, word 'walk' dropped.

11. Completing a passage

Here is one version of part of the passage you wrote in Exercise 7. What do you think the missing words might be? (One word in each space.)

Cockneys, people in the same . . . . . . class working in . . . . , have developed their own secret language, ... as 'Cockney rhyming slang'. . . . . . . Cockneys are Londoners, many of their . . . . . . expressions are associated with London; . . . . . . 'Chalk Farm' is the . . . . . . for 'arm'. Sometimes the last part of the rhyme* gets dropped, and as a . . . . . . it is often difficult for . . . . . . to understand the slang. . . . . . . the expression for 'head' is '. . . . . .', an abbreviation of the original 'loaf of bread'.

12. Describing an interview

Imagine that *you* were the person who interviewed Professor X. You now want to describe *briefly* – in an essay you are writing – what you asked him and how he replied. The essay is formal, so do not use the word 'I'.

Further reading

Ullmann S. *Words and their Use*, Frederick Muller, 1951.
Palmer F. R. *Semantics*, Cambridge University Press, 1976.
Leech G. *Semantics*, Penguin Books, 1974.
Ullman S. *The Principles of Semantics*, Blackwell, 1957.

Unit 14

Bread

Part I

1. Note-taking

Read this passage about bread, and complete the notes which follow it.

The discovery that the seeds* (or 'grains') of some plants can be eaten had an important effect on man's development. It made him realise that instead of spending all his time moving from place to place in search of animals to eat, he could actually stay in one place and grow some of his own food. It is no exaggeration to say that this discovery helped to turn man into an animal which settles* and forms a permanent home.

The grains of the wheat plant (in the form of a powder* known as 'flour') form the basic ingredient* of one of the world's most common foods – bread. The other ingredients of bread are yeast*, sugar, water, salt and fat.

In Europe, bread is usually made in five stages. The first is to make what is called 'dough'. The yeast is mixed with sugar and water, and after about fifteen minutes it begins to 'eat' the sugar. Flour, fat and salt are then put together and the yeast mixture is added. All these ingredients are then pressed (or 'kneaded') with the hands for about ten minutes until they form a large ball of dough. After the dough has been made in this way, it is left to 'rise'. As the yeast continues to eat the sugar it makes the dough increase in size, and this second stage of rising takes about two hours. At the third stage the risen dough is kneaded again and pushed into the shape the bread is to be. The dough must then be allowed to rise again, this time for about one hour. It is then ready for the final stage of baking*, which takes about forty-five minutes in a hot oven*.

In some countries the dough is not left to rise, the result being flat pieces of bread called 'unleavened (unrisen) bread'. Some religions of the world permit their followers to eat only unleavened bread.

How bread is made

Stage 1: . . . .
Stage 2: . . . .
Stage 3: . . . .
Stage 4: . . . .
Stage 5: . . . .

2. Vocabulary extension

Here are some words that could have been used in Paragraph 1 to make it more formal and academic. Decide where each expression could be used. Use a dictionary if necessary.

(i) edible*
(ii) is of great significance*
(iii) continually
(iv) it was possible
(v) one might even
(vi) transform
(vii) abode*

3. Writing instructions from a description

The passage *describes* how bread is made. Use this description to write a recipe, *giving instructions* on how to make bread. Begin:

First mix the yeast with the sugar and water. After about fifteen minutes it will begin to 'eat' the sugar. Then . . .

4. More about main topics

In Unit 13 you saw that the *main topic* of a sentence is usually mentioned in the first few words. Because most English sentences begin with the *subject*, we can say that the *subject* of a sentence usually mentions the *main topic*.

But if the *main topic* is mentioned in a part of the sentence that is not the subject, the writer may put that part of the sentence first.
For example:

> In some countries the dough is left to rise. In other countries they eat unleavened bread.

Here the writer is making a contrast between what happens *in some countries*, and what happens *in others*. Both sentences begin, not with the subject, but with an adverbial phrase.

Rewrite these sentences so they begin with a part of the sentence that is not the subject:

(a) The dough rises for two hours at the second stage. It rises for one hour at the fourth stage.
(b) It is forbidden in some religions to eat unleavened bread. It is not forbidden in other religions.
(c) Bread is usually made in five stages in Europe. Simpler types of bread are made in other parts of the world.
(d) The dough rises at the second stage. It is kneaded and shaped at the third stage.

10▶

Part II Describing a sequence of events

5. Here are two structures often used when describing sequences of events:

> After the dough has been made in this way, it is left to 'rise'. Before the dough is baked, it is left to rise again.

Use these structures to complete these sentences:

(a) After the dough has risen for two hours, ...
(b) Before the flour, fat and salt are mixed together . . . . . .
(c) After the dough has been kneaded again and pushed into shape . . . . . .
(d) Before . . . . . . , it is allowed to rise again.
(e) After . . . . . . , it is kneaded again and pushed into shape.
(f) After . . . . . . , it soon begins to 'eat' the sugar.

6. Here is another sentence describing a *sequence of events*:

> The yeast is mixed with sugar, which it soon begins to eat.

Notice that 'which' comes *immediately after* the word ('sugar') it refers to. Describe these sequences of events in the same way. Make sure 'which' comes *immediately after* the word it refers to.

(a) At the fourth stage the dough rises again. The fourth stage is followed by the baking stage.
(b) We make the dough at the first stage. The dough is then left to rise.
(c) The ingredients are kneaded by the cook. The ingredients form a large ball.
(d) Five stages are required in breadmaking. These five stages take about $4\frac{1}{2}$ hours to complete.
(e) Yeast is contained in the dough. Yeast makes the bread rise.

11▶

7. Writing a description from instructions

(i) Here are some instructions for cooking a very simple dish*, but the instructions are in the wrong order. First decide what dish is being described; then put the instructions in the correct order.

(a) Cook for about four minutes.
(b) Put some water into a saucepan*. Boil* it.
(c) Put egg (without shell) into cold water.
(d) Hold egg under hot tap for a few seconds. If put straight into boiling water the shell will break.
(e) Remove egg from water. Take off shell.
(f) Put egg into saucepan. Cover saucepan.

(ii) Write a description from the instructions given in (i).

8. Producing and distributing* bread

Because bread is such a popular food, its production and distribution is today a large industry. This diagram shows the stages in making and distributing bread. Write a paragraph describing this process.

Farm

Wheat is grown and cut. Grains are removed from it.

Mill*

Grains are made into flour.

Bakery*

Flour and other ingredients are made into bread. Packed and prepared for distribution.

Shop

Bread is sold to customers.

12▶

9. Writing about your subject

Write an essay describing a process associated with your own subject. Show it to someone in the class. He must make a table like the one completed in Exercise 1, showing *stages* in the process.

Part III Additional exercises

10. Reorganising a paragraph

Here is the writer's original plan for Paragraph 1 of the passage on page 78. One point mentioned in these notes is not mentioned in the passage itself. Which? How would you change the paragraph to mention this point?

Discovery grains could be eaten had important effect – man could stay in one place.

Reasons: (a) could grow some of own food. Not necessary to chase animals all time.
(b) grains don't perish* like meat. Can be stored* for winter (when animals hard to find).

∴ grains helped man to settle and form permanent home.

11. More about writing instructions

In all the descriptions of sequences in Exercise 5, the verb following 'after' or 'before' is in the passive. Here are two more structures using 'after' and 'before'. They are particularly useful when *giving instructions*.

After making the dough in this way, leave it to rise.
Before baking the dough, leave it to rise again.

Use these structures to make instructions from the descriptions in Exercise 5.

12. A dish from your country

Think of a dish which is common in your country. Write a description (*not* a recipe*) saying how the dish is made. Show it to someone else in the class. He must use your *description* to write a *recipe*. Check that his recipe is correct.

Further reading

McCance R. A. and Widdowson E. M. *Breads White and Brown*, Pitman Medical Publishing, 1956.
Jacob H. E. *Six Thousand Years of Bread*, Doubleday, Doran & Co., 1944.
Horder, Dodds C. and Moran T. *Bread,* Constable, 1954.

Unit 15 (Consolidation Unit)

The Spanish Armada

Part I

1. Completing a passage

Read this passage about the Spanish Armada. Some words (and sometimes whole sentences) are missing from it. Write down what you think the missing words might be.

In the late sixteenth century the Spanish Empire (1) . . . . . . and the Spanish king, Philip the Second, decided that the best way for him to defend his declining Empire was to attack England. He therefore (2) . . . . . . of the largest ships the world had seen, and called this fleet his Armada. There were 130 ships, with 7,000 sailors and 17,000 soldiers aboard. Another 30,000 Spanish soldiers were waiting in France. The plan was that the Armada (3) . . . . . . sail up the English Channel, destroying all the English ships it met. It would then guard the Spanish soldiers in France (4) . . . . . . to England on small boats.

The Armada was a disaster. As it entered the Channel the English attacked. (5) . . . . . . , the Spanish reached the point where they were to meet their soldiers in France. But then, at night, the English (6) . . . . . . – this time with 'fire boats'. These were boats filled with explosives and sent into the middle of the Armada. The Spanish tried to escape, sailing east. The English chased them up to Scotland, then left them. Slowly the Armada sailed round Scotland and back to Spain. Only about half the (7) . . . . . . number of ships reached Spain.

(8) . . . . . . ? The Spanish made one serious mistake. They thought the English ships would come close to fight. The Spanish – with their large number of soldiers and sailors – would then have won. But the English (9) . . . . Instead, as the Spanish entered the Channel, they attacked from a distance, and the Spanish ships, being so large, were easy to hit. (10) . . . . . . that the Spanish were far from home. As the English chased them towards Scotland, the Spanish began to run out of food and water, and there was nowhere for them to get more. Finally there was the weather. Storms hit the Armada on its return home down the west side of Britain. In fact storms did as much damage to the Armada as the English ships did.

The Spanish Armada

2. Here is the completed passage. Compare your words with the original ones, and discuss any differences. Then copy and complete the plan below the passage, saying *what happened* and *what went wrong*.

In the late sixteenth century the Spanish Empire was declining and the Spanish king, Philip the Second, decided that the best way for him to defend his declining Empire was to attack England. He therefore built a fleet* of the largest ships the world had seen, and called this fleet his Armada. There were 130 ships, with 7,000 sailors and 17,000 soldiers aboard. Another 30,000 Spanish soldiers were waiting in France. The plan was that the Armada should sail up the English Channel*, destroying all the English ships it met. It would then guard* the Spanish soldiers in France while they crossed to England on small boats.

The Armada was a disaster. As it entered the Channel the English attacked. In spite of this, the Spanish reached the point where they were to meet their soldiers in France. But then, at night, the English attacked again – this time with 'fire boats'. These were boats filled with explosives and sent into the middle of the Armada. The Spanish tried to escape, sailing east. The English chased them up to Scotland, then left them. Slowly the Armada sailed round Scotland and back to Spain. Only about half the original number of ships reached Spain.

Why was the Armada defeated? The Spanish made one serious mistake. They thought the English ships would come close to fight. The Spanish – with their large number of soldiers and sailors – would then have won. But the English did not come near. Instead, as the Spanish entered the Channel, they attacked from a distance, and the Spanish ships, being so large, were easy to hit. Then there was the fact that the Spanish were far from home. As the English chased them towards Scotland, the Spanish began to run out of food and water, and there was nowhere for them to get more. Finally there was the weather. Storms* hit* the Armada on its return home down the west side of Britain. In fact storms did as much damage to the Armada as the English ships did.

What happened (Paragraph 2)	**What went wrong** (Paragraph 3)
1. Spanish entered Channel.	1. English did not come close
2. Spanish reached meeting point. English	2. . . . .
3. Spanish tried to escape. English chased till Scotland.	3. . . . .
4.	4. Storms hit Armada.

3. Understanding the passage

Which of these sentences best describes the writer's *main point*?

In Paragraph 1, the writer:

(a) describes the great size of the Armada.
(b) explains why the Spanish Empire was declining.
(c) explains why Philip built the Armada, and describes his plan.

In Paragraph 2, the writer:

(a) describes what actually happened to the Armada.
(b) explains why the Armada was defeated.
(c) describes how the English fought the Armada.

How would you describe the *main point* the writer makes in Paragraph 3?

4. Revision

These sentences use some of the phrases you have learned in Units 11–14. Try to complete them.

Purpose and means

(a) Philip decided to defend his declining Empire by . . . . . .
(b) In order to escape, the Spanish . . . . . .
(c) The English attacked at night by . . . . . .

Prediction and expectancy

(d) The Spanish expected . . . . . . fight by coming close.
(e) The Armada should . . . . . . the Spanish soldiers in France,
(f) while they crossed to England. In fact . . . . . .

Cause, effect reason, result

(g) There was nowhere for the Spanish to get food and water. Consequently . . . . . .
(h) Because of the decline in his Empire, Philip . . . . . .

Describing a sequence

(i) After the English had attacked with fire boats, ...
(j) Before the Armada reached the point where they were to meet their soldiers, ...
(k) The English used fire boats to attack the Armada, which then . . . . . .

Part II Organising a description of events

5. In Paragraph 2 of the passage, the writer describes *what happened*, and in Paragraph 3 *what went wrong*. He could have written one paragraph doing both these things. Use the table you completed in Exercise 2 to write a short paragraph like this, saying what went wrong *as you are describing* what happened.

6. Sentence combining

Originally the Armada passage began with a paragraph which said these things. In which order? Decide, then join the sentences together to make a paragraph.

(1) An invader* must cross the water to reach Britain.
(2) The history of Europe is full of invasions*.
(3) The Spanish Armada failed.
(4) Neighbouring countries are the ones who invade*.
(5) Britain has escaped invasion partly because of its geographical position.
(6) In the past few centuries nearly every European country has been invaded.
(7) Britain is an island.
(8) The Spanish Armada is an example of an attempt to invade Britain.
(9) One of the few countries to escape recent invasion is Britain.

7. 'Operation* Sea Lion'*

In 1940 Germany planned to invade Britain. They called their plan 'Operation Sea Lion'. Write a paragraph about 'Operation Sea Lion', using this information:

A British General talking:

France has fallen. That means Britain is now Germany's main enemy. So they must invade. I'm sure they'll try this soon, and we must be prepared...

A German secret document:

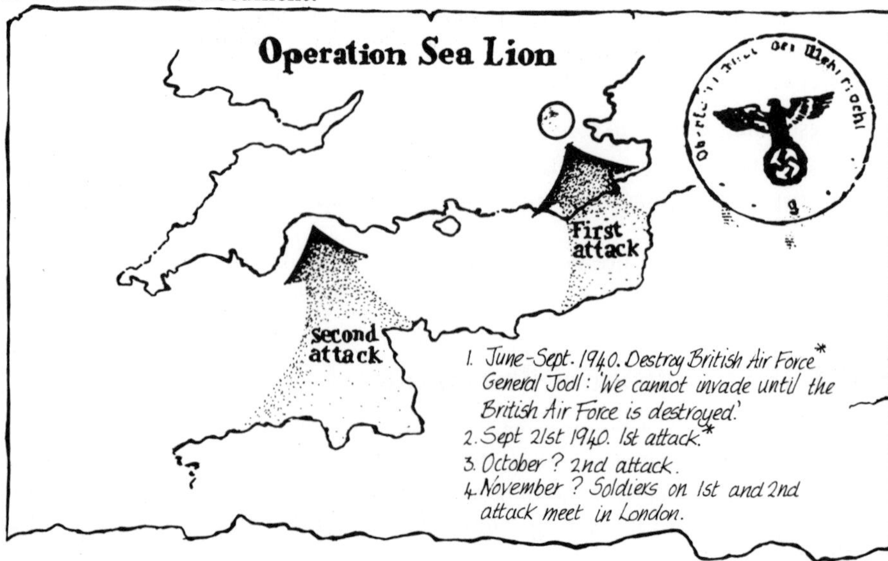

Operation Sea Lion
First attack
Second attack
1. June-Sept. 1940. Destroy British Air Force*
General Jodl: 'We cannot invade until the British Air Force is destroyed.'
2. Sept 21st 1940. 1st attack*
3. October ? 2nd attack.
4. November ? Soldiers on 1st and 2nd attack meet in London.

Unit 15

A British school teacher talking after the war:

Well, from June to September 1940 the German Air force attacked our Air Force and tried to destroy it. But they couldn't, and many German planes were destroyed. In fact in July we began to attack back. We attacked the German soldiers in France who were waiting to invade. Then in October, Germany decided to wait untill 1941 before invading. It was our Air Force which saved us.

8. Writing about your subject

In Units 11–14 you studied: expressing purpose and means; prediction and expectancy; cause, effect, reason, result; describing a sequence. Think of a sequence of events or a process associated with your own subject. Find out as much as you can about purpose, means, prediction, cause, effect, etc. and write an essay describing these things. Give your essay to someone in the class. Does he understand what you have written? If not, change the essay so that it is clearer.

Further reading

Mattingly G. *The Defeat of the Spanish Armada*, Penguin Books, 1959.
Bell D. *Drake*, Duckworth, 1935.
Fleming P. *Invasion 1940*, Rupert Hart-Davis, 1957.

Diagram referring to Unit 8, Exercise 8

The Egyptian invention for making holes

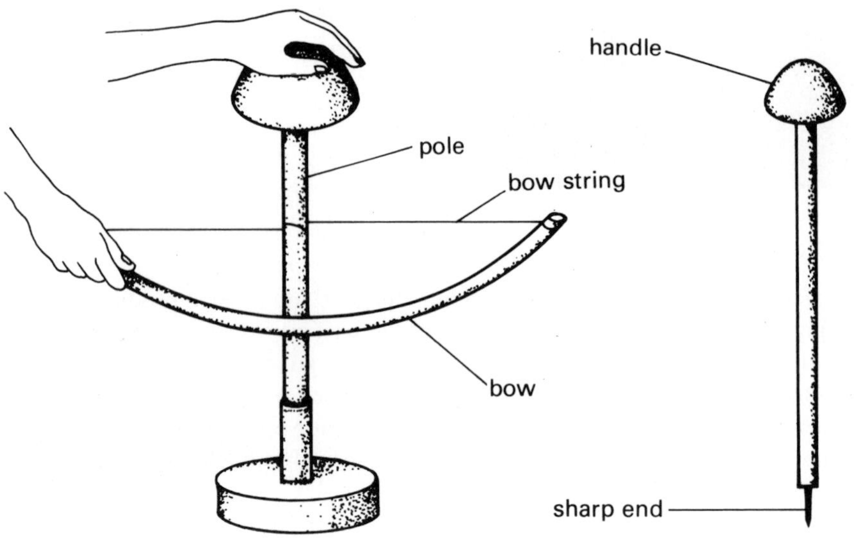

Words: vertical long thin
cylindrical attached to at one end

Part 3

Developing an argument

Unit 16

Women's Lib

Part I

1. In the 1960s a movement grew up in some countries (including Britain) called 'The Women's Liberation Movement' ('Women's Lib' for short). The movement believes that men have more rights* and opportunities than women. Its aim is to give women equality* with men. Do you think the passage below was written by someone who agrees or disagrees with Women's Lib?

Women in Britain are without doubt better off* today than they used to be. At the beginning of the nineteenth century women seem to have had almost no rights at all. They could not vote*, or even sign contracts*. Their marriages were arranged by their parents, and once they were married they could not own property. Most of the time they were kept at home, and even when they were allowed to work, they were never given responsible jobs. It is strange to think that, as far as we know, most women were happy with this situation.

Today the position is quite different. Women can now vote, and choose their own husbands. In 1970 a law* was passed* to give them an equal share of property in the case of divorce, and in the same year the Equal Pay Act* gave them the right to equal pay with men for work of equal value.

Yet despite these changes, there is no doubt that there are still great differences in status* between men and women. Many employers – maybe even the majority – seem to ignore the Equal Pay Act, and the average working woman is likely to earn only about half what a man earns for the same job. Most women who do work still do unskilled jobs, while only a small proportion of the country's workers – possibly one third – are in fact women. This small percentage is partly because of a shortage of nurseries*. If there were sufficient nurseries, up to twice as many women might well go out to work. There is also great inequality in education. Only a quarter of all university students are women, and at present boys' schools are undoubtedly much better than girls' schools.

2. Note-taking

Copy and complete these notes on the passage:

In 19th C. women:

(a) had no vote.
(b) couldn't sign contracts.
(c) . . . .
(d) . . . .
(e) . . . .
(f) . . . .

Today women:

(a) can vote.
(b) . . . .
(c) . . . .
(d) . . . .

Inequalities today:

(a) Work	(i)	Earn ½ what men earn for same job.
	(ii)	. . . .
	(iii)	Only small proportion work.
(b)	(i)	¼ univ. students women.
	(ii)	. . . .

3. Understanding the passage

Which of these descriptions best summarises the writer's *main point* in the passage? (Remember what you learned in Unit 6 about 'although'.)

(a) In the nineteenth century women were worse off* than today. Many improvements have been made.
(b) Although nineteenth-century women were worse off than women today, there are still many improvements to make.
(c) Although there are still many improvements to make, women in the nineteenth century were worse off than women today.

4. 'It is true that there are still many improvements to make. But women in the nineteenth century were worse off than today. Many improvements have been made.' Use the information given in the passage to write a short paragraph (about 150 words) putting forward this argument.

5. Emphasising a topic

If we wish to emphasise the topic of a sentence – when we are making a *contrast* for example – we can use the structure:

It is . . .	who which	. . .

The words after 'is' are the ones we are emphasising. For example, if we wish to emphasise that *women* (rather than *men*) do most unskilled jobs, we can write:

It is women who do most unskilled jobs.

Write sentences to emphasise that:

(a) In the nineteenth century *parents* (rather than sons and daughters) arranged the marriages.

(b) Today *women* (rather than *parents*) choose the husband.
(c) *A shortage of nurseries* (rather than anything else) makes so few married women work.
(d) *Boys*' (rather than *girls*') schools are much better.
(e) In the nineteenth century *men* (rather than *women*) signed all contracts.

Part II Expressing degrees of certainty

A writer often has to talk about facts and ideas which are not *certain*, but just *probable*, or only *possible*. It is important to be able to express the right *degree of certainty*. Imagine the reader's reaction if an unproved hypothesis is presented as a proved fact.

6. Here are some ideas taken from the passage. Does the writer say these things are *certainly*, *probably* or *possibly* true? Write down the words the writer uses each time to express degree of certainty.

(a) The position of British women is today better than it used to be.
(b) There are still great differences in the status of men and women.
(c) Girls' schools are today much worse than boys' schools.
(d) In the nineteenth century the majority of women were happy with their position.
(e) A working woman today earns about half what a man earns for the same job.
(f) With sufficient nurseries up to twice as many women would go out to work.
(g) A majority of employers seem to ignore the Equal Pay Act.
(h) One third of the workers in Britain are women.

7.

(i) When we think something is true but cannot be absolutely sure, we can express this by using the word 'seem'. Find two examples of this use of 'seem' in the passage.

(ii) Here is some information about woman's position today and in the past. Make sentences using 'seem' to express these ideas.

(a) Today many more women work outside the house.
(b) Woman's position has improved as the differences between the social classes have disappeared.
(c) Most of the changes in woman's position have taken place in the twentieth century.
(d) Societies have throughout history been dominated by man.
(e) Today woman's position is improving throughout the world.
(f) Until this century woman's position was roughly as it was five thousand years ago.

8. Misogynists

Sometimes the word 'misogynist' is used to describe someone who discriminates* against women. One American sociologist, Philip Goldberg, studied what sorts of people discriminate against women. Here are some of his findings:

PROBABLE : Mysogynous men are authoritarian*.
CERTAIN : Women as well as men can be mysogynous.
POSSIBLE : Mysogynous women come from unhappy families.
PROBABLE : Mysogynous men need to feel powerful.
CERTAIN : The average man and the average woman feel women cannot do certain important jobs.
POSSIBLE : Mysogynous men are neurotic*.
CERTAIN : Women are less certain than men about women's capabilities.

Write a paragraph describing Goldberg's findings. Make sure you express the right *degrees of certainty*. Before you begin to write, decide how you will organise the paragraph.

9. Women in England

Ms Y is a supporter of Women's Lib. In this interview she talks about the present and future position of women in England. Write a paragraph describing her views.

Q: Do you think there is discrimination against women in England today?

A: Certainly. Without any doubt. And not just in education and work either. In many other fields as well. The tax situation for women is very unfair for example.

Q: Are women better off in other countries then?

A: It depends on the country. There is certainly much less discrimination in Scandinavia, for example, and maybe in America too. But women are better off in England than in some countries. There's no question about that.

Q: Do you think the position of English women will improve?

A: In some ways it will, of course. I'm sure more women will go out to work in the next twenty years, and will earn more money. But women have a much greater problem than this to solve.

Q: What's that?

A: The problem of men's attitudes. We can earn more money in the future, but I'm not sure we can change men's attitudes. You see, most men – probably all – really think that women are inferior – the 'weaker sex'. Maybe we are physically weaker, but I don't think this means we are inferior. It'll be a hundred, possibly two hundred years before we can really change men's attitudes. Then there's another problem . . .

Q: Yes?

A: The problem of *women's* attitudes! Lots of women are unhappy with their present situation, but most of them probably don't want to fight for change.

It could be that Women's Lib has to spend more time changing women's attitudes than it spends in changing men's!

Q: I see. One last question. What about marriages? Some supporters* of Women's Lib believe that marriages should be abolished*. Do you agree?

A: No, I don't. It can't happen. What may (and should) happen is that we teach men to spend more time looking after the children and doing housework. And who knows? They might even enjoy it . . .

13▶

10. Writing about your subject

Every subject has controversial topics, on which different experts have different opinions. Think of a topic like this associated with your own subject. Write an essay about it, describing things which are *certainly, probably* and *possibly* true. Show what you have written to someone in the class. He must make a table, showing *degrees of certainty*.

Part III Additional exercises

11. Completing a passage

Here is how the passage on page 90 continues. What do you think the missing words might be? (One word for each space.)

There are still . . . . . . in Britain – though possibly nowadays a . . . . . . – who believe these . . . . . . reflect natural differences between men and women. 'A woman's place is in the home', they . . . . . . , and a woman has no . . . . . . to work outside the home, or . . . . . . to be educated. A woman, they . . . . . . say, is more . . . . . . than a man to bring up children, and if the mother goes out to work, the children will . . . . . . suffer. Such . . . . . . are false, and seem to be . . . . . . on the assumption that men and women are different at birth.

12. Women past and present

Use the information given in Exercise 7 to write a paragraph about the position of women *today* and *in the past*.

13. Women's Lib: your views

What do *you* think about woman's place in society? What do *you* think about Women's Lib? Write a short essay describing your views.

Further reading

Mitchell J. *Woman's Estate*, Penguin Books, 1966.
Morgan R. *Sisterhood is Powerful*, Random House, 1970.
Klein V. *The Feminine Character*, University of Illinois Press, 1972.
Denmark F. *Who Discriminates Against Women?*, Sage Publications, 1974.

Unit 17

Ghosts ... and other mysterious things

Part I

1. Read this passage about ghosts*. Do you think the writer believes in ghosts? What evidence do you have for your opinion?

According to a survey* done in the 1950s, one English person in every six believes in ghosts, and one in* fourteen thinks he has actually seen one. These figures are high, but in the sixteenth and seventeenth centuries almost everyone believed in ghosts.

The most common type of ghost is the poltergeist. This is a ghost which does not in fact appear. Instead, it makes noises and throws objects around. Yet despite this violent activity, poltergeists in fact never hurt anyone, as the case of the 'drummer* poltergeist' indicates. This was the first poltergeist recorded in Britain. In 1661 a beggar was put in prison for making a noise with his drum. The drum was taken away from him. But it continued playing by itself, and as it played objects were thrown about the room. Although the objects were hard and actually hit people, no-one was hurt. As one person present said: 'A piece of wool* could not have fallen more softly.' The drummer had another feature common to poltergeists: it could communicate. Someone asked it if it was the beggar who was making it play. He asked the drum to knock three times if the answer was yes . . . and it did!

There have been some very strange theories about ghosts. But most people believe that ghosts do not exist at all, and are just hallucinations in the minds of the people who 'see' them. There are several facts which point to this. One is that most ghosts appear only to people who knew the dead person, and when these people die themselves, the ghosts die with them. Also, as Colin Wilson points out, ghosts 'have a tendency to hang around* places they knew in life', because this is where the people who knew the dead person live. Ghosts should, Wilson continues, 'have something better to do'. A final piece of evidence comes from the fact that ghosts wear clothes! We may be able to believe in supernatural* people – people who come back from the dead. But supernatural clothes?

2. (i) Sentence combining

Here are some points which the writer makes in Paragraphs 1 and 2. In which order does he make them? Decide, then join the sentences together to make a summary of the paragraphs.

(1) Poltergeists throw objects around the room.
(2) In past centuries even more people believed in ghosts.
(3) Poltergeists can communicate with people.
(4) Some English people still believe in ghosts.
(5) The most common ghost is the poltergeist.

(6) Poltergeists rarely do harm.
(7) Poltergeists make noises.

(ii) Note-taking

In Paragraph 3 the writer gives three pieces of evidence for the theory that ghosts are hallucinations. Copy and complete these notes to show what that evidence is:

(a) Who they appear to: . . . . . .
(b) Where they appear: . . . . . .
(c) How they appear: . . . . . .

3. Adding information

(i) When the writer first wrote the passage, it included these sentences. Where in the passage do you think they appeared?

According to one writer, ghosts may be caused by radioactive* vibrations* sent from people who died long ago. After all, we are now receiving light from stars which shone many thousands of years ago. Just as these stars send light from the past, so perhaps people can also send light from the past.

(ii) You want to add this information to the sentences above. Decide *where* you would put it, and *what words* you would use.

(a) The name of the writer is A. M. W. Stirling.
(b) We are receiving the light from the stars only now because they are so far away.
(c) The people who send the vibrations probably had great radioactivity* in their bodies when they lived.
(d) Stirling admits the theory is a little fantastic.

4. More about emphasising a point

In Unit 16 you saw that we can emphasise part of a sentence (particularly when making a contrast) by using the structure 'It is . . .' Here is another structure you can use to emphasise part of a sentence (again, particularly when making a contrast):

What When How etc. . . .	is was etc.	. . .

e.g. A poltergeist does not appear. Instead what it does is make noises.

Here we are emphasising that a poltergeist makes noises (rather than appearing).

Use this structure to emphasise points in these sentences:

(a) Ghosts are probably not caused by radioactive vibrations. They may be caused by hallucinations.
(b) When asked a question, the drum did not keep silent. Instead, it knocked three times.
(c) Ghosts do not always do harm. Sometimes they help people.
(d) Ghosts do not appear everywhere. They appear near the places they lived.

***10*►**

Part II Supporting an argument

5.

(i) Here are some ways of *supporting an argument.* Find an example of each in the passage; say what argument is being supported, and write down the phrases the writer uses to introduce these different types of evidence.

(a) Supporting an argument by *giving an example*.
(b) Supporting an argument by *giving a quotation**.
(c) Supporting an argument by *mentioning a source** (without actually quoting from it).
(d) Supporting an argument by just *mentioning some facts*.

(ii) In line 22 of the passage, Colin Wilson is quoted. In fact, Wilson's actual words were something like this:

'A tendency to hang around places they knew in life shows how stupid ghosts are . . . one feels they ought to have something better to do.'

Notice how the writer of the passage takes only some of Wilson's words and puts them in sentences of his own.

6. Quoting someone

Here is what one writer, Dr X, says about the 'drummer poltergeist':

'A local judge*, John Mompesson, sent the beggar to prison, and took the drum back to his house. There it continued to play on its own. It also did other strange things. For example, one night Mompesson's children were lifted up in their beds. The drum even played little jokes, like hiding objects. Some people thought the whole thing was a trick* but so many people saw what happened that we cannot doubt it. These actions continued for a long time.'

Imagine that you are writing a passage about poltergeists. You have already mentioned the drummer poltergeist. Now you want to make the points below. Write sentences making each point and *supporting your argument* with a quotation from Dr X. Use phrases like 'according to Dr X . . .' and 'as Dr X says . . .'

(a) Poltergeists often do strange things.
(b) Poltergeists sometimes play jokes.
(c) Sometimes so many people see the actions of poltergeists that we cannot doubt that they happened.
(d) Sometimes the actions of poltergeists continue for a long time.

7. Foretelling the future

Can people foretell* the future? There is some evidence that they can. Look at these notes:

Some species of animals seem able to foretell the future. Some dogs seem to know when they are about to die.

No individual can foretell *all* future. Lyall Watson: 'If anyone were really able to predict the future . . . he would need only a year or two to become absolute ruler of the world.'

William Cox (American mathematician) tried to find out if groups of people could foretell train crashes. His findings: trains that crashed carried *much fewer* people than other trains.

In the 16th century a Frenchman, Nostradamus, foretold French Revolution. He even predicted the date.

Use this information to write a paragraph arguing that people can foretell the future. First write your plan. The paragraph should talk about *individual people*, *groups of people* and *man as a species*.

8. ETI

'ETI' means 'extra-terrestrial* intelligence'. Does it exist? Is there life on other planets? If so, is it intelligent . . . and can we communicate with it? Imagine you have to write an essay on these questions. Read the information below, plan your essay, and write it.

Stephen Dole (American astronomer) calculated: 640 million planets like earth in our galaxy*. At least a billion galaxies in the universe. A 50% chance of there being life on another planet less than 22 light years away.

Many attempts to communicate with ETI, e.g.:

(a) Frank Drake (American) tried to pick up* signals from space.
(b) American Jupiter rocket – 1970. Left with message aboard*. Will reach end of solar system* in 1984.

(c) 1974. Messages sent out from earth to a group of stars 24,000 light years* away. It will take 24,000 years for the message to reach the stars. Another 24,000 years for an answer to return!

People have always thought about ETI, e.g. Syrian writer Lucian wrote about the possibility 2 centuries before Christ.

Our solar system: 19th century astronomer William Herschel believed the sun could be inhabited.

Life on other planets is not necessarily intelligent. Biologists say it takes 4.6 billion years to reach intelligence.

Our solar system: American astronomer Abell says possibly on Jupiter 'but only Mars among the other planets is expected to have realistic chances of life'.

Will ETI be able to communicate with us? American astronomer Smith points out dolphins* are very intelligent, but have no technology*. 'Intelligence alone does not always result in the creation of a technical society.'

12▶

9. Writing about your subject

Think of a controversial topic associated with your subject. Write an essay supporting one point of view. If possible support the argument using all the ways mentioned in Exercise 5. Show your essay to someone in the class. He must recognise the different ways of supporting an argument you use.

Part III Additional exercises

10. Adding information

In the passage on page 96, the writer mentions three facts which suggest* that ghosts are hallucinations. Add a few sentences to the end of the passage to say what you would expect to be true if ghosts were not hallucinations.

11. Vocabulary expansion

Here are some expressions that Dr X could have used in the passage on page 98. Decide where each expression could be used, and rewrite the passage from line 3. Use a dictionary if necessary.

(i) an example of this is . . .
(ii) such as
(iii) considered
(iv) witnessed
(v) there can be no doubt . . .

12. Reaching a different conclusion

In Exercise 7 you wrote a paragraph arguing that people *can* foretell the future. Now write a paragraph arguing that people *cannot* foretell the future. Mention the evidence given in the notes; but your conclusion should be that this information is inconclusive.

Further reading

Watson L. *Supernature*, Hodder and Stoughton, 1973.
Steiner R. *Occult Science*, Rudolf Steiner Press, 1969.
Christian J. L. *Extra Terrestrial Intelligence*, Prometheus Books, 1979.

Unit 18

Genetic engineering

Part I

1. Read this passage about genetic* engineering. Which of these statements best describes the writer's attitude?

(a) There is no doubt that genetic engineering is a very attractive possibility.
(b) Genetic engineering seems to be an attractive possibility, but we must be cautious.
(c) Genetic engineering is not an attractive possibility; there are too many problems involved.

The study of genetics* is today so far advanced that we shall soon be able to produce a kind of genetically* perfect 'superman', using techniques known as 'genetic engineering'. At first this may seem an attractive possibility, but when we consider it in detail, we find there are many problems involved.

A distinction is usually made between 'negative' and 'positive' genetic engineering. In negative genetic engineering we try to eliminate harmful genes* to produce genetically normal people. The aim is of course a desirable one; however, it does pose the problem of what a harmful gene is. Genes are not really either 'good' or 'bad'. The gene which causes certain forms of anaemia*, for example, can also protect against malaria*. If we eliminate this gene we may get rid of* anaemia, but we increase the risk of malaria.

In positive genetic engineering we try to create better people by developing the so-called 'good' genes. But although this form of genetic engineering will give us greater control over mankind's future, there are several reasons for caution. First there is the possibility of mistakes. While accepting that geneticists* are responsible people, we must also admit that things can go wrong, the result being the kind of monster we read about in horror stories. Secondly, there is the problem of deciding what makes a 'better' person. We may feel, for example, that if genetic engineering can create more intelligent people, then this is a good thing. On the other hand, intelligence does not necessarily lead to happiness. Do we really want to create people who are intelligent, but perhaps unhappy?

The basic question is whether or not we should interfere with human life. We can argue that much human progress (particularly in medicine) involves interference with life. To some extent this is true; but we should not forget the terrible consequences genetic engineering can have. Consider for example the possibilities of genetic warfare*, in which our enemies try to harm us using the techniques of genetic engineering . . .

2. Note-taking

In the passage, the writer expresses some *reservations* about 'genetic engineering'. Copy and complete these notes showing what these reservations are.

Point	Reservation
1. Producing 'superman' an attractive possibility.	1. Many problems involved
2. Aim of neg. genetic engin. desirable.	2. . . . .
3.	3. Several reasons for caution.
4. Geneticists are responsible people.	4. . . . .
5. Creating more intelligent people a good thing.	5. . . . .
6. Much progress involves interference.	6. . . . .

3. Reorganising a paragraph

(i) In which order does the writer do these things in the last paragraph?

(a) Mentions one argument against interference.
(b) Mentions one argument for interference.
(c) States the general problem
(d) Gives an example to support the argument against interference.

(ii) In which order would you do these things if you began the paragraph like this?

'Genetic warfare, in which our enemies try to harm us using the techniques of genetic engineering, is today a possibility.'

Decide, then rewrite the paragraph.

4. Writing shorter sentences

(i) *Two short* sentences are sometimes better than *one long* sentence, which the reader may find difficult to follow. Here is one way of writing the first sentence of the passage as two sentences. Try to think of other ways.

> The study of genetics is today so far advanced that we shall soon be able to produce a kind of genetically perfect 'superman'. This can be done using techniques known as 'genetic engineering'.

(ii) Here are some more sentences from the passage. Make two shorter sentences each time.

(a) But although this form of genetic engineering will give us greater control over mankind's future, there are several reasons for caution.
(b) While accepting that geneticists are responsible people we must also admit that things can go wrong, the result being the kind of monster we read about in horror stories.
(c) We may feel, for example, that if genetic engineering can create more intelligent people, then this is a good thing.
(d) Consider, for example, the possibilities of genetic warfare, in which our enemies try to harm us using the techniques of genetic engineering.

9▶

Part II Expressing reservations

5.

(i) While accepting that geneticists are responsible people, we must also admit that things can go wrong.

In this sentence, the writer *makes a point* and *expresses a reservation*. Use the table you completed in Exercise 2 to *make points* and *express reservations* with 'while'.

(ii) In the sentence above, the writer uses 'while' to express his reservation. Write down the words he uses to express his reservations about the other points mentioned in Exercise 2.

6. Parallel writing

One method of discovering genetic diseases in babies is called 'screening'*. This means doing tests on large numbers of babies, to find the genetically abnormal* ones as early as possible. Here is a passage written by someone who does not believe in screening.

There are many problems with screening. First of all, it has to be done to a large number of babies. This makes it extremely expensive, and sometimes the result is to identify only one or two babies with genetic diseases*. Also, there is no point in screening babies for diseases with no cure, because in these cases we cannot benefit from discovering the disease. A final argument against screening is that if the child has a genetic disease we shall certainly find out anyway when at a later date the child shows symptoms.

Here are some reservations about these arguments:

Human life is important. Screening is worth the cost even if it identifies only one sick child.

Screening can save pain, even when there is no cure for the disease.
If we wait until the child shows symptoms, it may be too late for a cure.

Rewrite the passage from the point of view of someone who *believes* in screening. Mention the points made in the passage, in the same order; but your conclusion should be that screening is a good thing. Use some of the expressions you wrote down in Exercise 5(ii).

10▶

7. Genetic diseases

Here are two doctors talking about the differences between genetic diseases and other diseases. Write a paragraph about this, supporting Dr A's point of view, but expressing Dr B's reservations.

Dr A: There's no doubt that genetic diseases are very different from other diseases.
Dr B: Yes, there *are* differences, of course. But I'm not sure how important they are.
Dr A: OK. Well, let's look at the differences. First of all, genetic diseases are predictable. That's because they occur in the same families, from one generation to the next.
Dr B: Yes, that's true. But of course other diseases are predictable too. For example, if someone smokes too much, we can predict he may get cancer*.
Dr A: All right. But then there's the fact I just mentioned – that genetic diseases pass from generation to generation, not from individual to individual in the same generation.
Dr B: Yes, but some non-genetic diseases are the same. These are diseases which develop very slowly, and which parents give to their children.
Dr A: Yes, but these are rare.
Dr B: That's true, I suppose.
Dr A: Another point is that in most societies genetically deformed* people are considered 'inferior' . . .
Dr B: But that's true of some non-genetic diseases too. Take leprosy* for example. Most societies treat* people with leprosy as inferior!

11▶

8. Writing about your subject

Think of a controversial topic associated with your subject. Write an essay expressing one point of view, but *making reservations* to suggest why that point of view might not be entirely correct. Show your essay to someone in the class. He must make a table like the one completed in Exercise 2.

Part III Additional exercises

9. Completing a passage

Here is how the passage on page 102 originally began. What do you think the missing words might be? (One word for each space.)

The Ancient Greeks . . . . . . to put young babies onto the hillside, ... that the weakest died and only the strongest survived. This . . . . . . of the 'survival of the fittest' is, ... Darwin pointed out, the basis of evolution*. Indeed, ... one of Darwin's friends, Francis Galton, who first used the . . . . . . 'eugenics' for the . . . . . . of how we can control man's future by genetic means. Today we can talk of . . . . . . the fittest survive, not by putting babies on the hillside, ... by 'genetic engineering'. . . . . . . it will not be long before we can create genetically perfect . . . .

10. More about screening

The passage in Exercise 6 is written from the point of view of someone who *does not believe* in screening. Rewrite the passage from *the same point of view*, but mentioning the arguments in favour of screening.

11. A controversial subject

Work with a partner. Find a subject on which you and your partner have different views. Write an essay expressing *your* view, but mentioning *your partner's* reservations. Then compare your essays.

Further reading

Koller P. C. *Chromosomes and Genes*, Oliver and Boyd, 1968.
Beadle G. and Beadle M. *The Language of Life*, Gollancz, 1966.
Baer A. S. *The Genetic Perspective*, W. B. Saunders, 1977.

Unit 19

Work

Part I

1. Note-taking

Read this passage about work, then copy and complete the notes below it.

In recent years many countries of the world have been faced with the problem of how to make their workers more productive*. Some experts claim the answer is to make jobs more varied. But do more varied jobs lead to greater productivity*? There is evidence to suggest that while variety certainly makes the worker's life more enjoyable, it does not actually make him work harder. As far as increasing productivity is concerned, then, variety is not an important factor.

Other experts feel that giving the worker freedom to do his job in his own way is important, and there is no doubt that this is true. The problem is that this kind of freedom cannot easily be given in the modern factory* with its complicated machinery* which must be used in a fixed way. Thus while freedom of choice may be important, there is usually very little that can be done to create it.

Another important consideration is how much each worker contributes to the product he is making. In most factories the worker sees only one small part of the product. Some car factories are now experimenting with having many small production lines* rather than one large one, so that each worker contributes more to the production of the cars on his line. It would seem that not only is degree of worker contribution an important factor, therefore, but it is also one we can do something about.

To what extent does more money lead to greater productivity? The workers themselves certainly think this is important. But perhaps they want more money only because the work they do is so boring. Money just lets them enjoy their spare time* more. A similar argument may explain demands for shorter working hours. Perhaps if we succeed in making their jobs more interesting, they will neither want more money, nor will shorter working hours be so important to them.

Possible factors leading to greater productivity

1. Variety: makes life more enjoyable, but . . . . . .
2. . . . . . . : important, but . . . . . .
3. . . . . . . : . . . . . .
4. (a) . . . . . . }
   (b) . . . . . . } . . . . . .

2. Summarising

Use the notes you have completed to write a short summary of the passage.

3. Sentence combining

In the original version of the passage, the writer began by saying these things. Write a paragraph making these points:

(1) The relationship between managers and workers has changed in Britain.
(2) The relationship has changed since the Industrial Revolution.
(3) Many of the problems created by the Industrial Revolution are still with us.
(4) The Industrial Revolution was nearly 150 years ago.
(5) Industrial relations* in England are bad today.
(6) Why are industrial relations in England bad today?

4. Giving the same information in a different way

Here are two ways of giving the same information:

> In recent years many countries of the world have been faced with the problem of how to make their workers more productive. Some experts claim the answer is to make jobs more varied.
>
> In recent years many countries of the world have been faced with the same problem. This is the problem of how to make their workers more productive, and some experts claim the answer is to make jobs more varied.

Two sentences are used both times, but the second sentences begin at different places. Rewrite the short passages below. Use *only two* sentences each time, and begin the second at the line |:

(a) Other experts feel that giving the worker freedom to do his job in his own way is important,| and there is no doubt that this is true. The problem is that this kind of freedom cannot easily be given.
(b) There is evidence to suggest that while variety certainly makes the worker's life more enjoyable,| it does not make him work harder. As far as increasing productivity is concerned, variety is not therefore an important factor.
(c) A similar argument may explain demands for shorter working hours. Perhaps then if we succeed in making their jobs more interesting, they will neither want more money,| nor will shorter working hours be so important to them.
(d) In most factories the worker sees only one small part of the product. Some car factories are now experimenting| with having many small production lines rather than one large one.

Part II Drawing conclusions

5.

(i) Each paragraph of the passage contains one sentence in which the writer *draws conclusions*. Find these sentences, and notice the position of the words 'thus', 'therefore' and 'then' in them.

(ii) Not only is degree of worker contribution an important factor, therefore, but it is also one we can do something about.

The writer here draws two conclusions:

1. That degree of worker contribution is an important factor.
2. It is a factor we can do something about.

Notice that the words 'not only' are *immediately followed* by the verb. Draw more conclusions in the same way:

	Conclusion 1	Conclusion 2
(1)	Freedom of choice is important	Degree of worker participation is also important
(2)	Industrial relations in Britain	There is also low productivity in Britain
(3)	Modern factories have complicated machinery	It must also be used in a fixed way
(4)	Workers want more money	They also want shorter working hours

(iii) Perhaps they will neither want more money, nor will shorter working hours be so important to them.

Here the writer is again drawing two conclusions. Notice that the word 'nor' is *immediately followed* by the verb (which is *positive*). Draw more conclusions in the same way:

	Conclusion 1	Conclusion 2
(1)	Variety is not an important factor	It is not easy to make jobs more varied
(2)	There is not high productivity in Britain	Industrial relations are not good
(3)	The worker has no freedom in modern factories	He does not contribute much to the product he is making
(4)	In the past workers did not demand more money	In the past workers did not demand shorter working hours

10▶

6. 'A policeman's lot'*

(i) Here is a passage describing what two policemen think about their jobs. Write conclusions for each paragraph, saying which part of their work each finds *more* boring and *less* boring.

Policeman 1 said that as a young policeman he spent many hours walking the streets, and he found this very boring. However, he was then promoted* and now spends most of his time in an office. In fact he now remembers his street-walking days with great pleasure. . . . . . .

Policeman 2 also now spends most of his time in an office, and he admits that this can be boring. But, he says, when he remembers how as a young policeman he had to walk the streets, he considers how lucky he is today. . . . . . .

(ii) This is what Policeman 3 thinks. Add a paragraph to the passage above describing his point of view, and drawing his conclusion.

'The work a person is doing at the moment always seems particularly boring, and we often forget how boring work we did in the past was. I'm working in an office now, and it *is* boring. But then when I was walking the streets – that was boring too!'

7. Work and social class

In Britain there are great differences between the jobs of working class and middle class people. Use the information below to write a passage discussing these differences, with particular reference to social position, working conditions and future prospects.

The bus driver (working class)

Tom, aged 52, has been a bus driver since he was 18. He does not really enjoy his work, his main complaint being the bad working conditions. 'You spend all day sitting on a bus', he says, 'and that's very unhealthy.' When Tom was younger, he wanted to be an inspector*. But now he feels he is too old, and he only looks forward to his retirement*. How do other people consider his job? Most people consider bus drivers inferior, he says. 'They think it's unskilled work . . .'

The accountant* (middle class)

Q: What about your working conditions?
A: Oh, they're fine, actually. I work in an office, of course. It's big enough and I've no complaints.
Q: And prospects* for the future?
A: Well, if I stay with the company* I'm working for now, I'll probably be promoted in a couple of years' time. Or I could work privately. I'd certainly earn more money like that.

Q: What about social position? What do people say when they hear you're an accountant?
A: It's difficult to say really! I suppose most people consider me a professional, and think my kind of work is useful . . .

The solicitor* (middle class)

I enjoy my work very much. I think I'm doing a useful job, and other people seem to think so too. I'm hoping to work with one of the best-known solicitors in town soon. I'll certainly make lots of money if I do that. The thing I like best about my job is that I can choose my own working hours. I've got a new office in town, with a secretary, and things couldn't be better . . .

The factory worker (working class)

Q: What's the worst thing about your work?
A: I don't really know. I suppose the working conditions. It gets hot in the factory, really hot, and the noise is bad. After seven hours of that, I'm ready for a pint of beer, I can tell you.
Q: What do other people think about your job?
A: I think they're jealous, to tell the truth. I mean, they see my big car and they think, 'now where did he get the money to pay for that?'
Q: So you're well-paid, are you?
A: Oh yes. That's why I work – money! I'm not worried about prospects – there aren't any anyway – it's money I work for.

11▶

8. Writing about your subject

Think of a controversial topic associated with your subject. Write an essay describing several different points of view, and *drawing your own conclusions* on the topic. Show your essay to someone in the class. He must note down what your conclusions are.

Part III Additional exercises

9. Reorganising a paragraph

In Paragraph 4 of the passage on page 108, the writer discusses higher wages* and shorter working hours, in that order. Rewrite the paragraph so that shorter working hours are discussed first. Begin like this:

'To what extent do shorter working hours lead to greater productivity?'

10. Work and money

Everyone has opinions on the subject of higher wages. Some are given below. Use these opinions to write a short passage concluding *either* that higher wages are important, *or* that they are not. Whatever your conclusion, mention different points of view.

Do higher wages lead to better living conditions?

Yes, of course. The more money you have, the better you can live.
No. If everyone gets higher wages, the cost of living* rises.

Do higher wages give people a better position in society?

No. Position comes through education and through doing a useful job. Not through money.
Yes. Money buys bigger houses and better cars.

Do higher wages make workers content?

Of course they do. People work better if they feel they are paid enough.
No. If you give workers higher wages, they soon ask for even more money.

Do people really work for the money, or for something else?

For money. Many people actually choose to do boring jobs, if they are paid well.
Most people would rather have less pay and a more interesting job.

11. Your own work

Write an essay about your own career* (or future career), with particular reference to money, social position, working conditions and future prospects. Try to persuade the reader *either* that he should follow the same career, *or* that he should not.

Further reading

Fraser R. *Work*, Penguin Books, 1968.
Caplow T. *The Sociology of Work*, University of Minnesota Press, 1954.
Burns T. *Industrial Man*, Penguin Books, 1969.

Unit 20 (Consolidation Unit)

Intelligence

Part I

1. Read the first paragraph of this passage, *covering the rest of it with a piece of paper*. What do you think the writer is going to talk about next? Discuss in class. Then read the next paragraph and discuss the same question.

Are some people born clever, and others born stupid? Or is intelligence developed by our environment and our experiences? Strangely enough, the answer to both these questions is yes. To some extent our intelligence is given us at birth, and no amount of special education can make a genius* out of a child born with low intelligence. On the other hand, a child who lives in a boring environment will develop his intelligence less than one who lives in rich and varied surroundings. Thus the limits of a person's intelligence are fixed at birth, but whether or not he reaches those limits will depend on his environment. This view, now held by most experts, can be supported in a number of ways.

It is easy to show that intelligence is to some extent something we are born with. The closer the blood relationship between two people, the closer they are likely to be in intelligence. Thus if we take two unrelated people at random from the population, it is likely that their degrees of intelligence will be completely different. If on the other hand we take two identical twins*, they will very likely be as intelligent as each other. Relations like brothers and sisters, parents and children, usually have similar intelligence, and this clearly suggests that intelligence depends on birth.

Imagine now that we take two identical twins and put them in different environments. We might send one, for example, to a university and the other to a factory where the work is boring. We would soon find differences in intelligence developing, and this indicates that environment as well as birth plays a part. This conclusion is also suggested by the fact that people who live in close contact with each other, but who are not related at all, are likely to have similar degrees of intelligence.

2. Note-taking

Copy and complete these notes on the passage:

(i) Intelligence related to (a) . . . .
(b) . . . .

(ii) **Relationship between intelligence and birth**

Evidence: (a) . . . .
(b) . . . .

∴ . . . .

(iii) . . . .

Evidence: (a) . . . .

(b) . . . .

∴ . . . .

3. Understanding the passage

Decide which of these sentences best describes the writer's *main point.*

Paragraph 1

(a) To some extent, intelligence is given at birth.
(b) Intelligence is fixed at birth, but is developed by the environment.
(c) Intelligence is developed by the environment.

Paragraph 2

(a) To some extent, intelligence is given at birth.
(b) Unrelated people are likely to have different intelligence.
(c) Close relations usually have similar intelligence.

How would you describe the *main point* the writer makes in Paragraph 3?

4. Revision

These sentences use some of the phrases you have learned in Units 16–19. Try to complete them.

(a) While identical twins in the same environment have similar intelligence, ...
(b) Brothers and sisters are likely to . . . . . .
(c) According to most experts, ...
(d) Some people are born clever, and others stupid; however, ...
(e) As the case of identical twins in different environments indicates, ...

5. Persuading your partner

Work in pairs. You believe that birth is important for intelligence, and your partner believes that the environment is important. Write short passages to persuade the other person that his point of view is wrong.

Part II Organising an argument

6. Sentence combining

Here are some sentences about how intelligence is related to age. Join them together to make a paragraph.

(1) Most people reach their highest intelligence from 25–35.
(2) After 35, intelligence begins to lessen.

(3) The psychologist Wechsler points out that the intelligence of the average person of 50 is less than it was at 15.
(4) At around the age of 70 the decline in intelligence becomes very fast.
(5) Older men are not less able than younger men to carry out their lives.

7. Intelligence in town and country

(i) Many *argument passages* are organised like this:

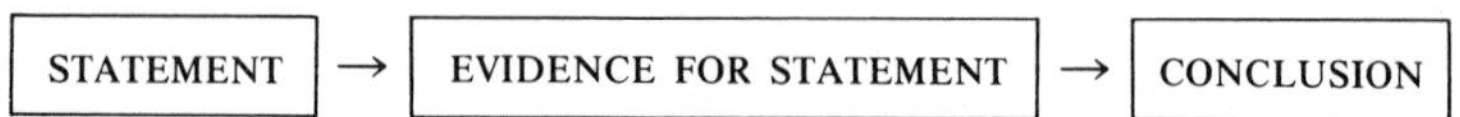

Which paragraph of the passage is organised like this?

(ii) The country is a more boring environment than the town. Here is some information about the intelligence of students living in a town and students living in the country.

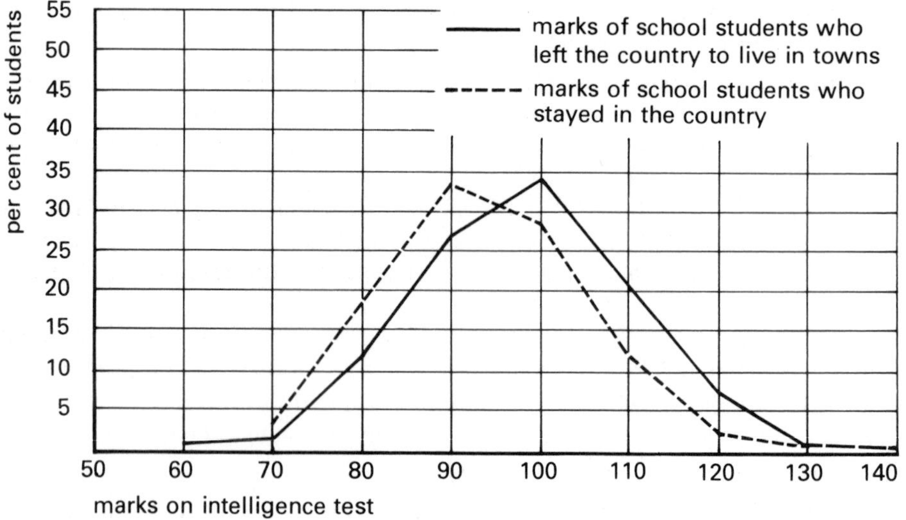

What conclusion would you draw from this information? Write a short paragraph about intelligence in town and country. It should be organised:

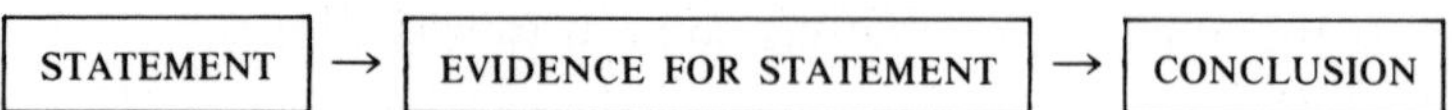

8. Introducing the topic

(i) Writers often begin argument passages with a few sentences just *introducing the topic*. Here are two sentences introducing a passage about race* and intelligence. Try to complete them. (One word for each space.)

What is the . . . . . . between intelligence and race? This is an . . . . . . of study which has . . . . . . particular public attention, because it is so . . . .

(ii) In Exercise 6 you wrote a paragraph about intelligence and age. Write a few sentences at the beginning of this paragraph to *introduce the topic.*

9. Intelligence tests

Psychologists have now created tests to find out how intelligent a person is. Dr A thinks these tests are bad, but Dr B disagrees. Write a paragraph mentioning Dr A's arguments, but supporting intelligence tests. Begin the paragraph with a few sentences to introduce the topic.

Dr A: Intelligence tests are very unfair. For one thing, how intelligent a person is is private information. Why should anyone else know?

Dr B: Oh, come on*. If you tell a person he's not very intelligent, it's like telling him he's got a bad heart. Before someone is given a job, he takes a medical examination. Why shouldn't his intelligence be tested as well?

Dr A: Perhaps, but a person is never told the result of an intelligence test. Why? Is it a secret?

Dr B: It's simple. Psychologists know that intelligence tests only give certain information. The ordinary person doesn't understand this. If a person knows he's done badly* on an intelligence test, he may take this too seriously. The results must be secret.

Dr A: Well, that's another thing. Intelligence tests only test one kind of ability. A person can have low intelligence, and be very clever in another way. He might be a great painter, for example. Intelligence isn't everything!

Dr B: Of course it isn't. But psychologists *know* this. There's nothing wrong with intelligence tests if we understand that they are testing *only* intelligence.

10. Writing about your subject

Think of a controversial topic associated with your subject. Write an essay so that someone who knows nothing about the subject will understand why the topic is controversial. Show your essay to someone in the class. If the person doesn't understand what you've written, make the essay clearer.

Further reading

Wertheimer M. *Fundamental Issues in Psychology*, Holt, Rinehart and Winston, 1972.

Resnick L. B. *The Nature of Intelligence*, Wiley, 1976.

Hilgard E. R. and Atkinson R. C. *Introduction to Psychology*, Harcourt, Brace and World, 1967.

Anastasi A. *Psychological Testing*, Macmillan, 1961.

Glossary

Unit 2

astronomers people who study stars

case example

collapse fall down or inwards; fall into pieces

consume use; use up

craters flat-bottomed steep-sided round holes on the moon's surface

density proportion of weight to volume

diameter (length of a) line going from one side to the other through the centre

equator imaginary line round the earth at an equal distance from its most northern and southern points

exposure being uncovered or made visible

going off exploding

helium kind of gas that is lighter than air and will not burn

let out send out; allow to escape

orbit move in a circle around (the earth)

rotation complete turn around a fixed point

swallowed made into a part of itself

telescope scientific instrument that makes distant objects seem larger and nearer

Unit 3

addicted unable to free oneself from a harmful habit

cardboard thick stiff paper material

charity help given to the poor – usually free food, clothing, etc.

freight goods; cargo

missionaries people who go to a certain place to spread their religion, often by doing good work for others

scavenger person who searches for usable objects among waste or unwanted things

skidded pushed so as to slip along the ground

slang words and expressions used by a particular group of people, not usually known to others

tramps people with no home or job who wander from place to place

Unit 4

beetles insects with two hard shiny cases which cover their wings when folded

centipedes small insect-like creatures with a long thin body with many joints, each joint having a pair of legs

clover small plant, usually with three leaves, often grown as food for animals

crabs sea creatures with a broad shell-covered body, four pairs of legs and a pair of strong claws for seizing food. Crabs walk sideways

crawl move with the body very close to the ground

fertile able to produce young

fertilise start the process of reproduction

grasshoppers insects with a thin body and long back legs, which make them able to jump high

hunters creatures which chase other creatures in order to catch and kill them for food

infertile unable to produce young

jostling pushing against each other (like people in a crowd)

lobsters large sea creatures with a shell-covered body, three pairs of legs and a pair of claws, whose flesh turns pink when cooked

locusts insects of Africa and Asia, which fly from place to place in large groups, often destroying crops

migrate move in a group from place to place, according to the seasons of the year

millipedes small worm-like creatures with a body with many joints, and very many legs

parasites creatures that live on other creatures and get food from them

shells hard outer coverings of some soft sea animals

shrimps small sea creatures with long legs and a long tail, whose flesh turns pink when cooked

species group of animals or plants of the same kind

spinning action of spider in making threads for a web

stinging having a small pointed part that can be used as a weapon

taken over controlled

tarantula large hairy poisonous spider

thread very fine cord made by spiders

transparent thin or fine enough to be seen through

trappers creatures that catch other creatures as food by making something that will hold them (e.g. spider's web)

trembling shaking

wagging moving the back part of the body from side to side

waist narrow middle part of the body

wasps yellow and black insects which fly and sting but do not produce sweet honey

webs nets of thin threads made by some insects, esp. spiders

Unit 5

admired considered beautiful

blowing away destroying by explosion

cabbage large round vegetable with many thick green leaves

cone top of a mountain which narrows almost to a point

derivation where a word comes from

earthquakes sudden shaking movements of the earth's surface

eruptions explosive movements which push out fire, rocks, etc.

flows moves in a liquid stream

glowing giving out bright light and heat, as from something burning

subject thing that is being written or spoken about

volcanoes mountains which sometimes explode

Unit 6

billion•a thousand millions; 1,000,000,000

clauses groups of words containing a subject and a verb

climate weather conditions usually found in a certain area

continent major land mass

distribution way of being spread out

exploited used or developed so as to get profit

explorers people who travel in unknown places to discover new things or places

fog thick substance like cloud which comes to the ground

freezing the temperature at which water becomes ice (0°C)

gallon a measure for liquids; 1 gallon = 8 pints or 4.54 litres

glaciers huge masses of ice which move slowly down mountain valleys

melt become water

m.p.h. miles per hour. Speed of movement measured in m.p.h.

polar regions areas around the most

northern and southern points of the earth

products goods; household articles

respect point; detail

seals large fish-eating animals that live by the sea, often hunted for their fur

stuck in trapped in; unable to move from

trade business of buying and selling

Unit 7

case in point example of what has been said

cure make well

damage harm

evil very bad

horns hard pointed growths on the head of certain animals

incest sexual relations between people in the same family

inoculation introduction of a weak form of a disease into the body as a protection against the disease

lightning flashes of light in the sky during a storm

lions large animals of the cat family found in Africa and Asia

lip one of the two soft outer edges of the mouth

magic power to make happen things that are not natural or normal

peas small green seeds which grow inside a long thin case, eaten as a vegetable

precautions things done to prevent something bad happening

reveal show; make known

stone hard natural substance; rock

thunder loud noise in the sky during a storm

tribe group of people made up of many families who share the same language, customs and social organisation

Unit 8

altar table or other raised object which is the most important place in a church or other religious place

arrow stick with pointed end (for showing a direction or particular place)

artificial done or made by man; not natural

attached (to) joined

bacteria living creatures too small for the eye to see, some of which cause disease

bent not straight; curved

bucket container for liquid, usually with a handle for carrying

cell one of the many very small pieces of matter of which all living things are formed

conical having a round, flat base and a point at the top

cultivating causing to grow and reproduce

cylinder object with two flat circular ends and parallel sides

cylindrical having two flat circular ends and parallel sides

drips (*verb*) falls in small drops

floats (*verb*) stays on top of the liquid without sinking

hollow empty inside

inherent forming a natural part (of a thing)

inspiration sudden clever idea

insulin chemical produced inside the body which controls the amount of sugar in the blood

inventions things made which did not exist before

inventor person who makes things which did not exist before

lead (to) result in

olives small green or black fruits which can give oil

penicillin medicine which kills many types of bacteria

pole long thin piece of wood or metal

primitive at an early stage of development; simple

ropes thick strong lines made by twisting several thinner pieces (of string) together

squeezing getting something out by pressing hard

steam mist or vapour which rises from boiling water

steam engine machine powered by the force of steam

steam turbine machine powered by the force of steam, often turning a wheel

tank usually large container for liquid

technological of the practical uses of scientific knowledge

temple religious building

tube long thin hollow pipe

vertical standing upright

winding (round) turning (something) many times round (something else)

Unit 9

acre unit of measurement of area, 4,840 square yards (approx. 4,000 square metres)

aristocrat person considered important in a society, often rich and powerful

beans seeds of certain plants used as a vegetable

bush small tree

calories units of measurement of heat, esp. the energy supplied by food

cocoa drink made from the powdered seeds of the cacao tree, from which chocolate is also made

comes from is made from

concentrated containing a lot (of the stated substance) in a small area

derived from comes from

drug any substance which has an effect on the body or mind

Dutch people of the Netherlands

energy (giving) bodily strength

fat oily substance found in animal and human bodies and in plants

filling something put inside, or between two parts of, something else

nervous system system of feeling and response in the body

relative clauses parts of a sentence that contain a subject and verb, and are usually introduced by the words *who*, *which* or *that*

source place where something starts; thing from which something else is made

stimulates increases the activity of; excites

(sugar) beet plant with a round, white root from which sugar is made

(sugar) cane plant with long, thick stems from which sugar is made

wheat plant which produces grain used for making flour, bread, etc.

Unit 10

accelerate / decelerate go faster/slower

acceleration / deceleration going faster/slower

astronaut person who travels in a space vehicle

centrifuge apparatus which spins something round very fast, so that a heavy object is forced outwards from the centre

consciousness normal state of being awake and knowing what is happening

deflect turn aside

depressurise change the specially controlled air pressure inside a vehicle

magnetic field area of effectiveness of a force that has the ability to attract metal to metal

Glossary

meteors pieces of solid matter travelling in space

ozone type of oxygen

protein food substance needed for good health

radiation force in the form of rays given out by some elements, which can harm living things

shield protection

short/long-term over a short/long period of time

space all that is outside the atmosphere of the earth

spaceship vehicle that travels in space

Unit 11

beaks hard horny pointed parts of a bird's mouth

circus performance (often in a tent) of various acts of skill and daring by people and animals

conditioned trained

experimenters people who make tests

experiments tests made in order to learn something

flashed shone or appeared for a moment

frame firm border or case

physiologist person who studies the bodies of living things

reflex action done, not on purpose, in reply to some outside influence

saliva natural watery liquid in the mouth

shaped influenced; determined

shaping determining a pattern of behaviour

technique skilled method

Unit 12

biological of living things

cave deep natural hollow place, usually underground

contact meeting; connection

cycles regularly repeated patterns

deprived (of) prevented from having

doubt consider unlikely

drug medicine or material used for making medicine

environment surrounding conditions

hypothesis idea which explains facts; theory

internal inside the body

oysters flat edible shellfish which produce pearls

predicate the part of a sentence which makes a statement about the subject

reflect in be shown in

task piece of work

tide regular rise and fall of the sea

Unit 13

attendant person who serves or looks after another

coach wheeled vehicle pulled by horses

common ordinary; having no special position or rank in society

dozens (of) lots of; many

dropped no longer used

endings letters added to the end of a word

expert person with special knowledge or skill

for one thing (used to introduce a reason, often as the first point in a discussion)

heavenly body large mass of matter in the sky (star, planet, etc.)

life guard someone or something that defends or protects

limbs legs, arms, or wings of an animal

loaf bread shaped and baked in one fairly large piece

rhyme (*verb*) end with the same sound

rhyme (*noun*) a short piece of writing using words which rhyme

undertakes agrees to do something; takes responsibility for doing something

Unit 14

abode home; place where someone lives

bakery place where bread is made

baking making bread

boil cause a liquid to reach the temperature at which water bubbles and changes into steam

dish amount of food of one kind cooked in a certain way

distributing taking or sending out to people who want to buy

edible fit to be eaten

ingredient necessary part of a mixture (esp. in cooking)

mill building that has a machine for crushing grain into flour

oven enclosed heated space used for cooking

perish become unfit to eat

powder very fine dry grains

recipe set of instructions for cooking a dish

saucepan deep, usually round, cooking pot with a handle

seeds small hard parts of a plant that can grow into a new plant

settles lives in one place

significance importance

stored kept for future use

yeast form of very small plant life, used for making bread light and soft

Unit 15

air force aeroplanes, men, etc., that are part of a country's military organisation

attack act of violence; going towards (a person or place) to fight

(English) Channel narrow sea passage between England and France

fleet group of ships under one command

guard protect; defend

hit come against with force

invade attack another country and take control of it

invader someone who invades

invasions acts of invading; being invaded

operation military action or movement

sea lion type of large fish-eating sea animal of the Pacific Ocean

storms rough weather with strong winds, rain, etc.

Unit 16

abolished brought to an end; stopped

Act law passed by parliament

authoritarian demanding obedience to rules whether or not they are right

better off in a better (financial) position

contracts legal agreements

discriminates (against) treats (someone) as being worse than others

equality being the same in rank

law rule made by the government and supported by the power of the police, etc.

neurotic suffering from a nervous disorder; not well balanced emotionally

nurseries places where small children are cared for while their parents work

passed declared to be law by the government

rights social, political and other advantages to which everyone has a just claim

status social position as seen by others

supporters people who approve of and encourage something

vote choose a representative in government at an election

worse off in a worse (financial) position

Glossary

Unit 17

aboard on or inside (a ship, train, spacecraft, etc.)

dolphins large intelligent air-breathing sea animals which swim about in groups

drummer someone who plays a drum

extra-terrestrial coming from outside the earth

foretell tell what will happen in the future

galaxy large group of stars

ghosts spirits of dead people who appear again

hang around stay near

judge (*noun*) person who decides questions in a court of law

light years distance that light travels in a year

one in (14) one out of every (fourteen)

pick up be able to hear or receive

quotation repeat of the words of another person or a book

radioactive sending out force in the form of rays which can harm living things

radioactivity radioactive force

solar system the sun together with the planets going round it

source place in a book, etc. where certain words or facts can be found; origin

suggest make one believe; point to the conclusion that

supernatural beyond the natural world

survey questioning a number of people chosen by chance, to find out opinions

technology practical use of scientific and other knowledge

trick something done to deceive or cheat

vibrations influences; power that can be felt but not seen

wool soft thick hair of sheep

Unit 18

abnormal not normal or usual

anaemia unhealthy condition of not having enough red cells in the blood

cancer diseased growth in the body

deformed having a body that is not normally shaped

diseases illnesses; disorders of the body

evolution scientific theory of the development of many varied species from a few simple ones

genes small parts in each cell in living bodies which control the qualities, development, etc. of that body and which have been passed on from parents

genetic of or concerning genes

genetically concerning genes; caused by genes

geneticists people who study genes

genetics the study of genes

get rid of destroy

leprosy disease in which the flesh, nerves and limbs are slowly destroyed

malaria disease of hot countries carried by certain types of mosquito

screening regular examining

treat act or behave towards

warfare fighting between different countries or groups

Unit 19

accountant person who examines money accounts of businesses, etc.

career profession; job which one intends to follow throughout one's life and for which one is trained

company business organisation

cost of living money needed for everyday necessities

factory building where goods are made in large quantities by machines

industrial relations the way workers and employers communicate with and understand each other

inspector official person who makes sure buses run on time, etc.

lot way of life; fate

machinery man-made apparatus that uses power (such as electricity) to perform work

production lines lines of machinery where each stage of an article's production is done in turn

productive making many things; doing much work

productivity rate of making things

promoted given a more important job

prospects chances of success

retirement time when one stops work because of age (usually 60–65)

solicitor person who deals with legal affairs

spare time time when one is not working

wages payment for work

Unit 20

come on (expression meaning: be reasonable; don't be foolish)

done badly (on) not done well; got a low mark

genius person of very high intelligence

race one of several divisions of people, each having a different body type

twins two babies born at the same time of the same mother

LONGMAN GROUP LIMITED
Longman House, Burnt Mill,
Harlow, Essex CM20 2JE, England
and Associated Companies throughout the World.

First published 1981
Fourth impression 1983

ISBN 0 582 74811 9

Acknowledgements

We are grateful to the following for permission to reproduce copyright material:
Adaptation of 'Heron's Steam Engine' from *Ancient Greek Gadgets and Machines* by Robert S. Brumbaugh (Thomas Y. Crowell Company, Inc.) Copyright © 1966 by Robert S. Brumbaugh. Reprinted by permission of Harper & Row, Publishers, Inc. for page 44; Reprinted from *Technology in the Ancient World* by Henry Hodges, published by Allen Lane, Penguin 1970, for pages 42, 45 and 118; Reprinted from 'Intelligence as a Selective Factor in Rural-Urban Migration' by Gist & Clark, *American Journal of Sociology 44 (1938/39)* by permission of Chicago Press, for page 116.
Holt, Rinehart and Winston Inc. for an adapted extract from *Fundamental Issues In Psychology* by Michael Wertheimer. Copyright © 1972 by Holt, Rinehart and Winston, Inc. Reprinted by permission.

Illustrations by Tony Baskeyfield

Phototypeset in Linotron 202 Times
Printed in Hong Kong by Sheck Wah Tong Printing Press Ltd.